Windows 8 XAML Primer

Jesse Liberty

Apress®

Windows 8 XAML Primer

ISBN-13 (pbk): 978-1-4302-4911-5

ISBN-13 (electronic): 978-1-4302-4912-2

Trademarked names, logos, and images may appear in this book. Rather than use a trademark symbol with every occurrence of a trademarked name, logo, or image we use the names, logos, and images only in an editorial fashion and to the benefit of the trademark owner, with no intention of infringement of the trademark.

The use in this publication of trade names, trademarks, service marks, and similar terms, even if they are not identified as such, is not to be taken as an expression of opinion as to whether or not they are subject to proprietary rights.

While the advice and information in this book are believed to be true and accurate at the date of publication, neither the authors nor the editors nor the publisher can accept any legal responsibility for any errors or omissions that may be made. The publisher makes no warranty, express or implied, with respect to the material contained herein.

President and Publisher: Paul Manning

Lead Editor: Ewan Buckingham

Developmental Editor: Ewan Buckingham

Technical Reviewer: Andy Olsen

Editorial Board: Steve Anglin, Ewan Buckingham, Gary Cornell, Louise Corrigan, Morgan Ertel, Jonathan Gennick, Jonathan Hassell, Robert Hutchinson, Michelle Lowman, James Markham, Matthew Moodie, Jeff Olson, Jeffrey Pepper, Douglas Pundick, Ben Renow-Clarke, Dominic Shakeshaft, Gwenan Spearing, Matt Wade, Tom Welsh

Coordinating Editor: Katie Sullivan

Copy Editor: Mary Behr

Compositor: Bytheway Publishing Services

Indexer: SPi Global

Artist: SPi Global

Cover Designer: Anna Ishchenko

Distributed to the book trade worldwide by Springer Science+Business Media New York, 233 Spring Street, 6th Floor, New York, NY 10013. Phone 1-800-SPRINGER, fax (201) 348-4505, e-mail orders-ny@springer-sbm.com, or visit www.springeronline.com.

For information on translations, please e-mail rights@apress.com, or visit www.apress.com.

Apress and friends of ED books may be purchased in bulk for academic, corporate, or promotional use. eBook versions and licenses are also available for most titles. For more information, reference our Special Bulk Sales–eBook Licensing web page at www.apress.com/bulk-sales.

Any source code or other supplementary materials referenced by the author in this text is available to readers at www.apress.com. For detailed information about how to locate your book's source code, go to www.apress.com/source-code.

This book is dedicated to my daughters. I could not be prouder.

—Jesse Liberty

Contents at a Glance

Foreword...vii

About the Author viii

About the Technical Reviewer...ix

Acknowledgments..x

Chapter 1: XAML For Windows 8: Read Me First...1

Chapter 2: Data Binding 17

Chapter 3: Panels...27

Chapter 4: Controls..37

Chapter 5: Styles and Templates 61

Chapter 6: Animation and Visual State..71

Index 81

Contents

Foreword..vii

About the Author viii

About the Technical Reviewer..ix

Acknowledgments x

Chapter 1: XAML For Windows 8: Read Me First..1

Writing Programs With XAML 1

    Creating Your First XAML Application 1

    Stack Panel..4

    Event Handling...6

    Improving the Layout with Grid Rows and Columns 7

Windows 8 and Layout 11

    Positioning and Sizing 11

    Available Space 12

    Padding...12

    Alignment 13

    Layout Conventions 13

Adding Controls and Setting Properties 14

Chapter 2: Data Binding 17

Binding to Objects 17

Three Data Binding Modes 19

Binding and INotifyPropertyChanged..19

Binding to Other Elements...22

Binding and Data Conversion 23

Binding to Lists..24

■ **Chapter 3: Panels**..**27**

Canvas..28

Stack Panel 30

Grid..31

WrapGrid...34

Border...35

■ **Chapter 4: Controls**..**37**

TextControls...37

Selection Controls...41

Content for Controls..43

Shapes..51

Presentation Controls..53

■ **Chapter 5: Styles and Templates** **61**

Based on Styles..62

Implicit Styles..63

Templates 64

■ **Chapter 6:Animation and Visual State**..................................**71**

From-To Animation 71

Key-frame Animation...72

Easing...75

View State 76

■ **Index** **81**

Foreword

"In keeping with the intentions of this book of getting to the heart of the matter—and not wasting your time—I will not review the history of XAML nor the theory of XAML nor will I tell you why XAML is a great markup language. Instead I'll turn immediately to writing programs for Windows 8 using XAML."
These are the first sentences that you're going to read when you get to the first chapter of this book. And these sentences tell you everything that you need to know about both this book and the author.

The book tackles the major issues that you'll need to understand in order to get started if you're a XAML and C# programmer that wants to get down to business building your first Windows 8 apps. Does it tell you about the new UX requirements? No. Does it teach you C#? No. Does it mess around with unnecessary editorials on the importance of Windows 8 in rebooting the developer ecosystem with 400M pairs of eyeballs (800M eyeballs altogether) looking for your apps? No! It assumes that you've done your share of the umpteen Microsoft marketing presentations that lay out the fluff and are ready to get down to the gruff. He lays out what the tools are, how to use them, and how to sling the code you need to do on Windows 8: using the project templates in both Visual Studio and Blend, making something useful appear on the screen, binding your data to your controls, laying out your data on the screen, styling your data, and animating the display of your data.

Is it the whole story? No. That would take 800 pages. This is the first 100 pages you need to get started.

And what about the author? Is he qualified to decide on your first 100 pages? Absolutely.

Jesse Liberty is known for doing some of the most popular of everything he does: writing, speaking, podcasting. And he specializes in communicating all things XAML, including WPF, Silverlight, Windows Phone 7, and now Windows 8/XAML. Telerik was proud to hire him at the beginning of 2012 and we're jealous of the time you get from him writing this book (luckily he decided to give up sleeping while writing this book or we'd be really upset). He's one of those guys that gets talked about in hushed tones, "You get to work with Jesse Liberty? What's he really like?"

You have in your hands the first 100 pages you need from the man that's best able to give it to you. Enjoy.

Chris Sells
Vice President, Developer Tools
csells@telerik.com
http://sellsbrothers.com

About the Author

 **Jesse Liberty** is a Technical Evangelist for Telerik. Liberty hosts the popular Yet Another Podcast and his blog (http://JesseLiberty.com) is required reading. He is the author of numerous best-selling books, including the forthcoming *Pro Windows 8 Development with XAML and C#* (Apress, 2013). He was a Senior Evangelist for Microsoft, Distinguished Software Engineer at AT&T, Software Architect for PBS, and Vice President of Information Technology at Citibank. Jesse can be followed on Twitter at @JesseLiberty.

About the Technical Reviewer

 **Andy Olsen** runs a software training company based in the UK, delivering training in .NET, Java, web and mobile technologies in Europe, the US, and Asia. Andy has been working with .NET since the days of the first beta and is actively involved with the latest features of the .NET 4.5 platform. Andy lives by the sea in Swansea with his wife, Jayne, and their children, Emily and Tom. Andy enjoys running along the seafront (with lots of coffee stops along the way), skiing, and following the Swans! You can contact Andy at andyo@olsensoft.com.

Acknowledgments

As is always true, this book could not have been created without the incredible help from the folks at Apress, especially Katie Sullivan, Ewan Buckingham, Andy Olsen, and Mary Behr. I also appreciate the support I received from Telerik (www.Telerik.com).

—Jesse Liberty

■ ■ ■

CHAPTER 1

XAML For Windows 8: Read Me First

Writing Programs With XAML

It is the intention of this book to get to the heart of the matter—and not waste your time—so I will not review the history of XAML (pronounced "zamel," It rhymes with "camel"), nor the theory of XAML, nor will I tell you why XAML is a great markup language. Instead I will turn immediately to writing programs for Windows 8 using XAML. While XAML is also the markup language for WPF, Silverlight, Windows Phone, and other technologies, this book focuses on XAML for Windows 8 and assumes that you have already installed Windows 8 and Visual C#. Note that it does not matter which version of Visual Studio/ Visual C# you are using.

■ **Note** Even if you have not programmed in C# before, you should be able to follow all of the examples in this book, though this is not a primer on C#. If you prefer, you may want to keep a C# primer on your desk for easy reference. I recommend Introducing *C#* by Adam Freeman (Apress) or *Learning C# 3.0* by Jesse Liberty and Brian MacDonald(O'Reilly).

Creating Your First XAML Application

Open Visual Studio and select New Project. In the New Project dialog, look in the left pane and expand Templates ➤ Visual C# ➤ Windows Store. This is how you will create every program in this book. In the right hand pane, select Blank App (XAML). Give the application a name and click OK, as shown in Figure 1-1.

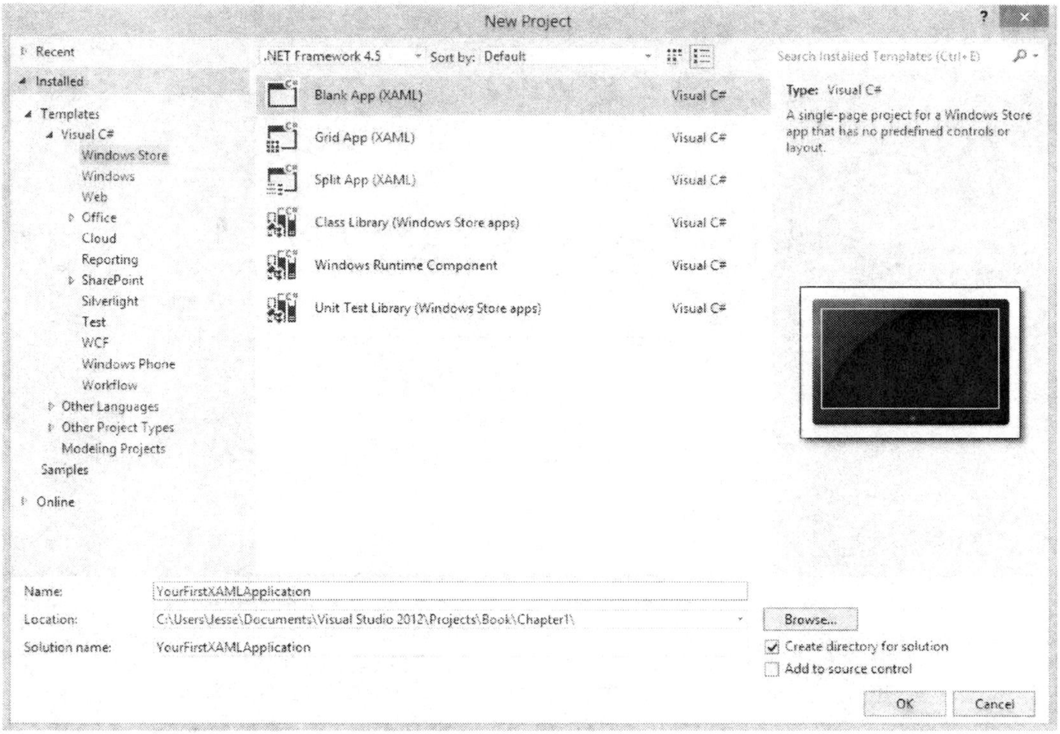

Figure 1-1. Visual Studio's New Project dialog

When your application opens, double-click `MainPage.xaml` in the Solution Explorer (which will appear as a pane on the right side of your workspace). `MainPage.xaml` is where you'll work for most of this book. What you are looking at is XAML, the default XAML that Visual Studio puts into the `MainPage` of your application.

```
<Page
    x:Class="YourFirstXAMLApplication.MainPage"
    IsTabStop="false"
    xmlns="http://schemas.microsoft.com/winfx/2006/xaml/presentation"
    xmlns:x="http://schemas.microsoft.com/winfx/2006/xaml"
    xmlns:local="using:YourFirstXAMLApplication"
    xmlns:d="http://schemas.microsoft.com/expression/blend/2008"
    xmlns:mc="http://schemas.openxmlformats.org/markup-compatibility/2006"
    mc:Ignorable="d">

    <Grid Background="{StaticResource ApplicationPageBackgroundThemeBrush}">

    </Grid>
</Page>
```

The first element is of type `Page` and it represents the page itself. On line 2, the class for this page (`MainPage`) is identified, complete with its full namespace (see the "XML Namespaces" sidebar). Because the Page is a control, its default setting for IsTabStop is true. Since you don't want the page itself to be in the list of tab stops in the page, you set IsTabStop to false.

This is followed by the identification of a number of useful namespaces. Note that most have the syntax xmlns:namespaceName such as xmlns:local or xmlns:x but the first (http://schemas.microsoft.com/winfx/2006/xaml/presentation) does not have the colon and namespace prefix and thus is the default namespace for controls on this page.

XML NAMESPACES

Generally, namespaces are a way to divide up and segregate the identifiers used in a program. In XAML, XML namespaces are often used to differentiate controls from different vendors. For example, when you declare an instance of a TextBlock, you are really defining an instance of the TextBlock control provided by Microsoft, as identified in the default namespace. It is possible and legal (if confusing) to declare a TextBlock in your own library, and the two will be distinguished by the XML namespace prefix.

If you purchase third party controls (such as those sold by Telerik and other vendors), the controls will be referenced through the vendor's namespace, such as <telerik:RadSlider> and this namespace will be identified at the top of the page with a statement like

```
xmlns:telerik="using:Telerik.UI.Xaml.Controls"
```

This declares the namespace telerik for use in the remainder of the page.

Below the namespace definitions is the declaration of a Grid. A Grid is one of numerous types of panels (see Chapter 3) that you can use in XAML to organize the layout of the controls on your page. A Grid typically has rows and columns defined. In this case, however, no rows or columns have been defined yet so the default Grid consists of a single giant cell.

The background color for the Grid is set to a StaticResource named ApplicationPageBackgroundThemeBrush. Static resources will be described in detail later (see Chapter 5), but they are a common way to reuse resources such as brushes and styles. In this case, you are setting the background of the grid to whatever color is stored in ApplicationPageBackgroundThemeBrush.

In order to see anything interesting when you run this application you must add at least one display control to the Grid. There are many ways to do this, as you'll see throughout the book. For now, you'll type the XAML directly into the XAML editor.

Notice that the Grid (like all elements) has an open and a close tag. The close tag is just like the open tag except that it begins with a forward slash and has no attributes.

```
</Grid>
```

Every element must have a close tag, though it is legal for elements to be self-closing.

```
<TextBlock Text="Hello" />
```

You'll place the control inside the Grid by placing it between the opening and closing tags. To get started, you'll use a TextBlock element, which is designed to display text. Each element can take a number of attributes for detailing how the text is displayed; you'll use just a few.

```
<Grid Background="{StaticResource ApplicationPageBackgroundThemeBrush}">
    <TextBlock
        Text="Hello World"
        FontFamily="Segoe UI"
        FontSize="45"
```

```
            FontWeight="SemiBold" />
    </Grid>
```

The effect of this (which you can see on the design surface, and especially when you run the project by pressing Control-F5) is to display the words "Hello World" in the font family, size, and weight designated by the attributes, as shown in Figure 1-2.

Figure 1-2. Hello World

Stack Panel

For all the fun of being able to display text, there isn't much excitement until the user can interact with what is on the screen. TextBlock has a close cousin, TextBox, that gathers text from the user. Let's create a very small data entry form using a few TextBlocks, TextBoxes, and a Button in a new project named "A small form." You'll arrange these on top of one another (and in some cases next to one another) using the StackPanel, as shown in Figure 1-3.

Figure 1-3. A small form

Here is the XAML for the form in Figure 1-3:

```xml
<Page
    x:Class="A_small_form.MainPage"
    IsTabStop="false"
    xmlns="http://schemas.microsoft.com/winfx/2006/xaml/presentation"
    xmlns:x="http://schemas.microsoft.com/winfx/2006/xaml"
    xmlns:local="using:A_small_form"
    xmlns:d="http://schemas.microsoft.com/expression/blend/2008"
    xmlns:mc="http://schemas.openxmlformats.org/markup-compatibility/2006"
    mc:Ignorable="d">

    <Grid Background="{StaticResource ApplicationPageBackgroundThemeBrush}">
        <StackPanel VerticalAlignment="Stretch" HorizontalAlignment="Stretch">
            <StackPanel Orientation="Horizontal" VerticalAlignment="Stretch"
HorizontalAlignment="Stretch" Margin="5">
                <TextBlock
                    Text="Your Name "
                    FontSize="40"
                    VerticalAlignment="Bottom"
                    Margin="5"/>
```

```xaml
            <TextBox
                Name="Name"
                Width="300"
                Height="60"
                FontSize="40" />
        </StackPanel>
        <StackPanel
            Orientation="Horizontal"
            VerticalAlignment="Stretch"
            HorizontalAlignment="Stretch"
            Margin="5">
            <TextBlock
                Text="Your Phone"
                FontSize="40"
                VerticalAlignment="Bottom"
                Margin="5" />
            <TextBox
                Name="Phone"
                Width="300"
                Height="60"
                FontSize="40" />
        </StackPanel>
        <Button
            Name="ProcessForm"
            Content="Process"
            Height="60"
            Width="300"
            FontSize="40"
            Click="ProcessForm_Click_1" />

        </StackPanel>
    </Grid>
</Page>
```

▨ **Note**   While you can download all the source code from the Apress web site, I strongly recommend typing in the code to better learn the material. You can save some keystrokes, however, by using the properties window (described below) to fill in the properties of various controls.

This is a considerably more complex set of code. You are not using the rows and columns of the grid, but rather you've placed a StackPanel directly into the grid. A StackPanel, as its name implies, stacks one object atop or next to another. The default orientation for a StackPanel is vertical (one on top of another) but you can set it to horizontal.

Inside your StackPanel you placed two more StackPanel (with horizontal orientations) and a Button. The effect, as shown in Figure 1-3, is to have an outer stacked panel with two inner stacked panels, and then a button below.

The inner StackPanels are marked with orientation set to horizontal, and inside each is a TextBlock and a TextBox, aligning these two next to one another. The StackPanels have their vertical and horizontal alignments set. The possible values for horizontal and vertical alignment are from enumerated constants (e.g., Left, Center, Right, Stretch) and thus are shown by IntelliSense (Microsoft's implementation of autocompletion), making coding with these values easier. You'll find that IntelliSense is pervasive in Visual Studio programming of XAML.

Notice that the TextBoxes have Name attributes; this allows you to refer to them in the code. Any XAML object that is given a name can be referred to in the code. However, you do not have to declare controls in the code; the XAML declaration is enough to establish the name of the object. You'll see this in just a moment when you examine the event handler for the button click event. Each TextBox also has its Width and Height set as the TextBox does not (yet) have text, and thus cannot size itself automatically.

At the bottom of the outer-most StackPanel you've added a Button. It too has a name, as you'll refer to it in code, and a Width, FontSize, etc. The Button has a Content attribute, which can be any form of content, though the most common is to use a string with the text you want to appear in the Button.

Event Handling

Entering text, however, won't do much good unless you can do something with the text that is entered. This is where event handling comes in.

The Button also has an event, Click, and when you add the Click event, Visual Studio also adds an event handler. If you allow Visual Studio to do so, it will name the event handler for you and create a stub of the event handler in the codebehind file. The codebehind file has the same name as the XAML file but with the extension .cs for C# or .vb for Visual Basic.

When the button is clicked, the event is raised and the event handler is called. Open MainPage.xaml.cs and you'll see the stubbed out event handler. You want a place to put the text you pick up from the TextBoxes, so let's add one more TextBlock below the button, as follows:

```
<TextBlock
    Name="Message"
    Margin="5" />
```

This TextBlock does not have a Text property (initially it will be blank) but it does have a Name property as you'll be updating the content of the Text property programmatically.

Let's turn to the event handler in the codebehind file. To open the codebehind file, click the arrow next to MainPage.xaml in Solution Explorer to expose MainPage.xaml.cs and double-click that file to open it. When you open the file, you'll notice that there are three methods already in place.

```
public sealed partial class MainPage : Page
{
    public MainPage()
    {
        this.InitializeComponent();
    }

    protected override void OnNavigatedTo(NavigationEventArgs e)
    {
    }

    private void ProcessForm_Click_1( object sender, RoutedEventArgs e )
    {
    }
}
```

The first method (named for the class) is the constructor, which initializes all the controls and runs before any other method. The OnNavigatedTo method is called when you navigate to the page (which you do in this case just by starting the application). It is very common to put code into this method to set up the page. The third method is the stub for your event handler. This was created when you created the event, and now it is time to fill in the logic for the event handler. All you will do, in this case, is pick up the entries from the two TextBoxes and place their data into the Message TextBlock.

Before you begin adding code to the event handler, notice that the event handler has two parameters. This is true of all event handlers. The first parameter is the object that raised the event, called sender. In this case, sender will be the button whose click event was raised. The second parameter is either of type RoutedEventArgs or a type derived from RoutedEventArgs. A simple RoutedEventArgs argument has nothing in it, but the derived types can have information that is very valuable when handling the event.

```csharp
private void ProcessForm_Click_1( object sender, RoutedEventArgs e )
{
    var name = Name.Text;
    var phone = Phone.Text;
    var message = string.Format( "{0}'s phone number is {1}", name, phone );
    Message.Text = message;
}
```

In this event handler, you first extract the values from the Name and Phone TextBoxes and then you concatenate them in a local string variable named message. Finally, you assign message to the Text attribute of the Message TextBlock. I broke it out this way for clarity, but you can write it in a single line of code:

```csharp
Message.Text = string.Format( "{0}'s phone number is {1}", Name.Text, Phone.Text );
```

Note   For the sake of clarity, I will most often use the more verbose form in coding throughout this book. This way, if things don't go as expected, it is far easier to set break points and examine the value of each variable in turn.

Before leaving this example, notice that the XAML elements Name, Phone, and Message were available in the C# without explicit declaration. Declaration in the XAML was sufficient to declare these in the C#, and so they could be referenced and used in the code.

Notice also that, because C# is case-sensitive, there is no confusion between *message* (lower case), which is the local variable holding the string, and *Message* (upper case), which is the control that will display the string. That said, there can be *human* confusion when you use the same name for more than one thing and so it may have been better programming practice to name the local variable *msg*.

```csharp
var msg = string.Format( "{0}'s phone number is {1}", name, phone );
Message.Text = msg;
```

Improving the Layout with Grid Rows and Columns

You may have noticed in Figure 1-3 that while the StackPanel did the job and was very convenient, in this case the result was not as gratifyingly attractive as it might have been. The TextBoxes did not line up properly and things looked a bit sloppy.

You can fix that with margins and padding, but a cleaner and easier way is to use the Grid as it was intended, with rows and columns, placing your controls into individual cells. To do this, you must first declare the rows and columns themselves, together with their respective sizes. Each row or column can have its dimensions set using a number of different measures. The three most common, however, are

- Absolute sizing

- Relative (star) sizing
- Automatic sizing

With absolute sizing, you define the height or width with as a number of pixels, just as you did in the previous example.

With relative sizing, you describe what fraction of the height or width each row will have. Relative sizing can be a bit confusing at first, so let's take an example. To indicate a relative size, you add a star (asterisk) after the value. Thus you might write

```
<Grid.RowDefinitions>
    <RowDefinition
        Height="2*" />
    <RowDefinition
        Height="*" />
</Grid.RowDefinitions>
```

In this case, you have set up a 2:1 size ratio (a star with no number is equivalent to 1*). Whatever the height of your application, the first row will be twice as high as the second. If there are 900 pixels available, then the first row will be 600 pixels and the second row 300.

If you add a new first row that is marked as 3*, then you will have the ratio 3:2:1, and thus you get 450 pixels, 300 pixels, and 150 pixels if your total is 900. Whatever the size of your window, however, the proportions will be 3/6 to the first row, 2/6 to the second row and 1/6 to the third, as shown in Figure 1-4.

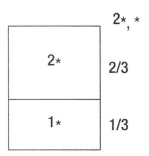

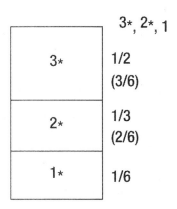

Figure 1-4. Ratios and resulting real estate

Automatic sizing uses the keyword Auto to indicate that the row ought to take up whatever size is required for the controls in that row, but no more. It is not uncommon to see something like this:

```
<Grid.RowDefinitions>
    <RowDefinition
        Height="Auto" />
    <RowDefinition
        Height="*" />
</Grid.RowDefinitions>
```

This code will cause the first row size to be big enough for its controls, and the second row to take up all the remaining room.

You'll learn a good bit more about sizing as you continue. For now, you simply want to size your two prompts, a button, and the output message. You want the prompts to take up 1/3 of the width of the grid, and the answers to take up the remaining 2/3. To place an object in the first row (offset 0), use the designation

```
grid.row = "0";
```

To place an object in the second column (offset 1), use the designation

```
grid.column = "1";
```

The default is for the row and column to be zero, but it is best to be explicit and set the grid row and column for each control even in row and/or column zero.

■ **Note** The class name changes from example to example: that is because the downloadable code breaks these into separate projects. If you are continuing on in the same project, be sure to fix the class name at the top of the XAML and the namespace in the codebehind.

```
<Page
    x:Class="Grid_Layout.MainPage"
    IsTabStop="false"
    xmlns="http://schemas.microsoft.com/winfx/2006/xaml/presentation"
    xmlns:x="http://schemas.microsoft.com/winfx/2006/xaml"
    xmlns:local="using:Grid_Layout"
    xmlns:d="http://schemas.microsoft.com/expression/blend/2008"
    xmlns:mc="http://schemas.openxmlformats.org/markup-compatibility/2006"
    mc:Ignorable="d">

    <Grid Background="{StaticResource ApplicationPageBackgroundThemeBrush}">
        <Grid.RowDefinitions>
            <RowDefinition
                Height="Auto" />
            <RowDefinition
                Height="Auto" />
            <RowDefinition
                Height="Auto" />
            <RowDefinition
                Height="Auto" />
        </Grid.RowDefinitions>
```

```xaml
        <Grid.ColumnDefinitions>
            <ColumnDefinition
                Width="*" />
            <ColumnDefinition
                Width="2*" />
        </Grid.ColumnDefinitions>
        <TextBlock
            Grid.Row = "0"
            Grid.Column = "0"
            Text="Your Name "
            FontSize="40"
            VerticalAlignment="Bottom"
            Margin="5" />
        <TextBox
            Grid.Row = "0"
            Grid.Column="1"
            Name="Name"
            Width="300"
            Height="60"
            HorizontalAlignment="Left"
            Margin="5"
            FontSize="40" />
        <TextBlock
            Grid.Row="1"
            Text="Your Phone "
            FontSize="40"
            VerticalAlignment="Bottom"
            Margin="5" />
        <TextBox
            Grid.Row="1"
            Grid.Column="1"
            Name="Phone"
            Width="300"
            Height="60"
            HorizontalAlignment="Left"
            Margin="5"
            FontSize="40"/>
        <Button
            Grid.Row="2"
            Name="ProcessForm"
            Content="Process"
            Height="Auto"
            Width="Auto"
            FontSize="30"
            Click="ProcessForm_Click_1" />
        <TextBlock
            Name="Message"
            Margin="5"
            FontSize="20"
            Grid.Row="3"/>
    </Grid>
```

```
</Page>
```

The default grid row and column is zero and zero, respectively (that is, first row and first column). You'll notice that the prompts (and button) do not designate the column. While this works, I actually don't encourage it (and show it here only to demonstrate that these are the defaults). It is usually better to be explicit in naming the grid row and column for each element to make maintenance easier (easier-to-understand code is easier to maintain).

Notice that I changed the height and width of the button to Auto, thus sizing it to the contents of the button. The result of running the code is shown in Figure 1-5.

Figure 1-5. The new and improved grid

■ **Note**   Grid rows and columns are zero-indexed. Thus the first row is Grid.Row = 0 and the second row is Grid.Row=1.

Windows 8 and Layout

With Windows 8, your application must run on a diverse set of display devices from small slate computers to state-of-the-art high-resolution monitors. While the lower limit is 768x1024, below a width of 1366 pixels the ability to create a split is disabled. Note that aspect ratios vary significantly, with some monitors being much wider with respect to their height than others. In other words, you cannot safely predict what the aspect ratios your application will encounter.

In addition to supporting the various screen resolutions, your application will need to look good in both landscape and portrait mode. With the movement of Windows to slate computers, changing the orientation of the screen is simple, common, and frequent.

Positioning and Sizing

Critical to the positioning of elements within a panel is the size of the element. Typically you can use the intrinsic size of the element, but at times you'll want to set the height and width explicitly.

Most common is to use "size to content" where the element's size is determined by the size of what it contains. For example, a text element would be sized to fit the assigned text, taking into account the length of the text, the size of the font, etc. On the other hand, you might choose to set the width of a text element, letting the text wrap and thus ensuring the horizontal alignment you might need on a page.

Often you will not need to or be able to set the width or height of an element because its dimensions are constrained. For example, a Text element inside a Grid view might be constrained by the size of the cell it occupies. The outer panel (e.g., the Grid) might well be constrained by the size of the device it is running on.

While you may want to allow controls such as buttons and text elements to size to their content, you may also want to impose arbitrary limits on their minimum or maximum size. Setting, for example,

MinHeight and MinWidth can avoid the problem of having touchable controls that are too small for a finger to touch accurately.

Because the operating system may be forced to override even your minimum sizes (so that the element stays on the screen) you can inquire for the *actual* sizes with ActualWidth and AcutalHeight. You can read these in an event handler for the LayoutUpdatedEvent to ensure that you are getting the current value

Available Space

Each element is allocated a certain amount of space, called the *layout slot*. If the element is set to size to content, the space available may exceed the space needed. You can position your element within the layout slot in a number of ways. One way, and the most direct, is to set a margin on the element, as shown in Figure 1-6.

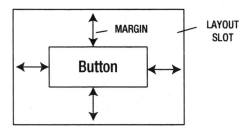

Figure 1-6. Setting a margin on the element

You can set a top margin, a margin for left or right, or a margin for the bottom. If you set the margin to just one number like this

```
Margin="5"
```

a margin of 5 pixels will be set all around the object. However, if you provide two values, like

```
Margin="10,20"
```

the first value will be split between the left and right margin (thus, in this case, a margin of 5 each) and the second number will be split between the top and bottom margins.

Finally, you can explicitly set the margin for all four positions, in the order of Left, Top, Right, Bottom. Thus, if you want a margin of 5 on the left and 10 on the bottom but zero on top and right, you would set

```
Margin = "5,0,0,10"
```

Padding

Padding is very similar to margins in many respects, but it affects the amount of space *within* an element that has text. For example, a button typically has text content, and padding that determines how much space surrounds that text within the button itself. You can set the padding in the same way you set the margin (a single number, a pair of numbers, or four numbers), as shown in Figure 1-7.

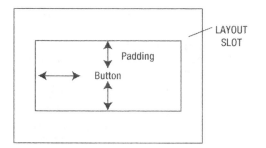

Figure 1-7. Padding

Alignment

You can also position an element within the available space using the VerticalAlignment and HorizontalAlignment. Thus, if you set a button to size to content but the area available for that button is bigger than the button itself, these alignment settings will determine where in the available area the button (with its margin) is positioned.

The possible settings for HorizontalAlignment are Left, Center, Right, and Stretch; for vertical alignment the settings are Top, Center, Bottom, and Stretch. If Stretch is set, the element will be stretched to fill the available space.

Alignment can be used across different controls to cause their tops to align, while padding is most often used to provide space between a border and whatever is inside the border, and a margin is typically used to reposition the control within its assigned space. All of these can be combined to provide the exact look you desire.

Layout Conventions

The UI design guidelines provide guidance on how to layout your application so that it not only looks professional but so that it is consistent with other Windows 8 applications. Microsoft's guidelines suggest restricting yourself to four font sizes of 42, 20, 11, and 9 (with 42 reserved for page headers, 20 reserved for sub-headers, 11 for navigation and text, and 9 for secondary information, labels, and so forth). The most common font for Windows 8 applications is Segoe UI, though other Segoe variants are used. The relative font sizes are shown in Figure 1-8.

Figure 1-8. Relative font sizes

Further, the guidelines state that you should align everything in your UI to a grid based on units of 20 pixels. The goal is for all shapes, and in particular rectangles, to align with the (imaginary) gridlines. Similarly, text baselines should fall on the gridlines.

■ **Note**   In Microsoft's documentation, 20 pixels is referred to as a unit.

You can turn on gridlines in Visual Studio by clicking on the Gridlines button at the bottom of the Design surface, as shown in Figure 1-9.

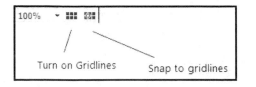

Figure 1-9. Gridlines button

Headings should be on a unit line, five units from the top. Remembering that a unit is 20 pixels, this means that your heading should be 100 pixels from the top. Your content should be seven units from the top (140 pixels). Typically you will achieve these alignments by using the built-in templates and by setting margins on controls rather than by using absolute positioning on a canvas.

Adding Controls and Setting Properties

There are numerous ways to add controls to the design surface and to set their properties. The most direct, but also the approach requiring the most experience with XAML, is to add the control directly to the XAML code itself. For example, for the Grid for the MainPage of your new application you might write the following code:

```
<Grid Background="{StaticResource ApplicationPageBackgroundThemeBrush}">
    <TextBlock
        Margin="100,40,0,0"
        Text="Hello World"
        FontFamily="SegoeUI"
        FontSize="40" />
</Grid>
```

Another approach, however, would be to open the design surface and drag a TextBlock onto the design surface from the Toolbox. You can then set the properties (attributes) on the TextBlock from the Properties window (typically found on the right side of the design surface, below the Solution Explorer), as seen in Figure 1-10.

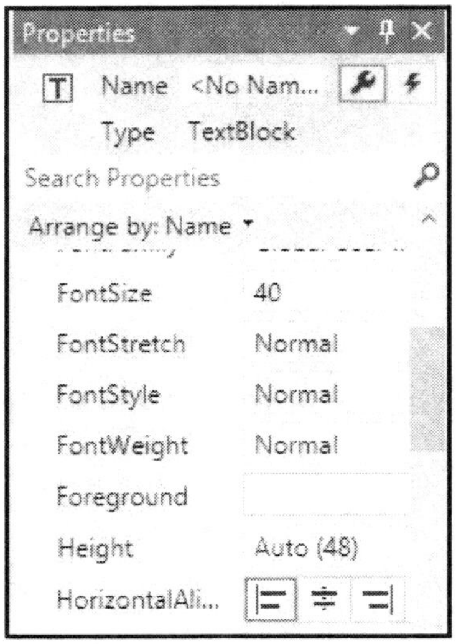

Figure 1-10. *The properties window (excerpt) for the TextBlock*

You are of course free to mix and match, dragging from the Toolbox and then editing in the XAML, declaring in the XAML and then editing from the Toolbox, even dragging from the Toolbox directly onto the XAML!

Notice that as you change properties in the properties window, the attributes are immediately updated in the XAML, and vice versa; as you update the XAML, the properties window is updated. These are two views of the same information.

░ **Note**   A third approach is to use Blend, which I will cover later in this book.

To keep things simple, I'll often show the XAML for a control, but feel free to create that XAML by dragging the control from the Toolbox and setting its properties in the Properties window. In fact, that is very good practice—real programmers do use design surfaces.

CHAPTER 2

■ ■ ■

Data Binding

Data binding is often thought of as an advanced topic, but there really is no reason for that. Data binding is:

- Critical to writing XAML applications
- Not very difficult to learn
- A very powerful technique

The basic idea behind data binding couldn't be simpler: you are going to provide values to UIElements based on the values of objects or of other UIElements.

■ **Note**　UIElement is a base class for most of the objects that have a visual appearance and can process input in Windows 8 applications.

Binding to Objects

Let's take the first case first: binding an UIElement to an object. The target of the binding must be an UIElement, but the source of the binding can be any POCO (Plain Old CLR Object). In other words, the source can be just about anything.

■ **Note**　When we talk about the target of binding, we mean the control that has a value bound to it. When we talk about the source of binding, we mean the object that has the value from which we will bind.

For example, if you have an object that represents a person, and that Person object has two public properties, Name and Age, you may want to bind those properties to TextBlocks so that you can display them easily without hard-coding the values. In that case, the Person object (POCO) is the source and the TextBlocks (UIElements) are the targets of the binding.

To create this binding, you set the appropriate property (in this case Text) of the UIElement using the syntax of {binding <property>} where <property> is Name, Age, or whatever the public property is. The following code provides a very simple illustration. You begin by declaring an object to which you can bind; this is a POCO object.

```
class Employee
{
    public string Name { get; set; }
    public string Title { get; set; }

    public Employee(string name, string title)
    {
        Name = name;
        Title = title;
    }

    public static Employee GetEmployee()
    {
        var emp = new Employee( "Tom", "Developer" );
        return emp;
    }

}
```

As you can see, the Employee class has two public properties. You bind to these properties in the XAML.

```
<StackPanel Name="xDisplay">
    <StackPanel
        Orientation="Horizontal">
        <TextBlock
            Text="Name:" />
        <TextBlock
            Margin="5,0,0,0"
            Text="{Binding Name}" />
    </StackPanel>
    <StackPanel
        Orientation="Horizontal">
        <TextBlock
            Text="Title:" />
        <TextBlock
            Margin="5,0,0,0"
            Text="{Binding Title}" />
    </StackPanel>
</StackPanel>
```

Note For this and all XAML examples, please place the XAML shown within the default Grid on the MainPage unless the example indicates otherwise.

The code indicates that you want to bind to the Name and Title properties, respectively, but of which object? It may be that there are many Employee objects around at any given moment. The answer is found in the DataContext. This can be set in the XAML or in the code; here you set it in code, in MainPage.xaml. cs:

```
protected override void OnNavigatedTo(NavigationEventArgs e)
{
    xDisplay.DataContext = Employee.GetEmployee();
}
```

The DataContext says "I promised you a value in various properties. Please obtain those properties from *this* object."

Every UIElement has a DataContext property. You can assign each individually, or you can, as I've done here, assign a DataContext further up the visibility tree (in this case, on the StackPanel). The DataContext will be "inherited" by all the UIElements further down the tree unless they have their own DataContext, in which case it will override the ancestor's DataContext.

Three Data Binding Modes

When data binding, you can designate one of three data binding modes:

- OneTime
- OneWay
- TwoWay

These determine whether and when the control is updated based on changes to the underlying data and vice versa. With OneTime binding, the control is not updated even if the underlying data changes. It is rare to use OneTime binding, but it can be useful in taking a snapshot of the state of a database at any given moment. With OneWay binding, the UI is updated when the underlying data changes, but updating the UI has no effect on the underlying data. With TwoWay binding, changes made to the underlying data are reflected in the UI and changes made by the user in the UI are reflected in the underlying data (and presumably persisted, for example to a database).

If you want TwoWay binding on the TextBlock for Name, you could use the following code:

```
Text="{Binding Name, Mode=TwoWay}" />
```

■ **Note**   The default is OneWay binding.

Typically, TextBlocks are bound with OneWay binding as they are read-only, and TextBoxes (which are read/write) are bound with TwoWay binding.

Binding and INotifyPropertyChanged

Earlier I said that with OneWay binding (and TwoWay, for that matter), the UI is updated when the underlying data changes. This is true, but you have to help it along. You do so by having the class that you are binding to implement INotifyPropertyChanged. This interface has only one event, PropertyChanged. You raise this event each time a property is set in your class, and as a result, the UI is notified and updated.

The classic implementation tests to see if anyone has registered with the event, and if so raises the event using the object itself as the sender and creates a new NotifyPropertyEventArgs object with the name of the property as the argument to the constructor.

Typically, this is all factored out to a helper method called RaisePropertyChanged in the following code. The UI is dead simple—just TextBlocks to hold the prompts for Name and Title, and more TextBlocks to display the (bound) values. The button at the bottom of the StackPanel has an event handler, which will change the value of Name (simulating a change coming from a server). Because of INotifyChanged, when the value of Name changes, it will be immediately reflected in the UI.

```xml
<StackPanel Name="LayoutRoot">
    <StackPanel
        Orientation="Horizontal">
        <TextBlock
            Text="Name" />
        <TextBlock
            Margin="5,0,0,0"
            Height="50"
            Width="200"
            Text="{Binding Name}" />
    </StackPanel>
    <StackPanel
        Orientation="Horizontal"
        Margin="0,5,0,0">
        <TextBlock
            Text="Title" />
        <TextBlock
            Margin="5,0,0,0"
            Height="50"
            Width="200"
            Text="{Binding Title}" />
    </StackPanel>
    <Button
        Name="xChange"
        Content="Change"
        Margin="0,5,0,0"
        Click="xChange_Click_1" />
</StackPanel>
```

The Employee class implements INotifyPropertyChanged.

■ **Note**   As you can see, some of the terms in the class will have red squiggly lines under them. Place the cursor on that term, and type control-dot. Visual Studio will offer to add the missing namespace for you. Presto! Your code works.

```csharp
class Employee  : INotifyPropertyChanged
{
    private string _name;
    public string Name
    {
        get { return _name; }
        set
        {
            _name = value;
            RaisePropertyChanged();
```

```
        }
    }

    private string _title;
    public string Title
    {
        get { return _title; }
        set
        {
            _title = value;
            RaisePropertyChanged();
        }
    }

    private void RaisePropertyChanged(
        [CallerMemberName] string caller = "" )
    {
        if ( PropertyChanged != null )
        {
            PropertyChanged( this, new PropertyChangedEventArgs( caller ) );
        }
    }

    public event PropertyChangedEventHandler PropertyChanged;
}
```

Finally, the codebehind for MainPage.xaml has the event handler for the button.

```
public sealed partial class MainPage : Page
{

    Employee emp = new Employee() { Name = "George", Title = "President" };
    public MainPage()
    {
        this.InitializeComponent();
    }

    protected override void OnNavigatedTo(NavigationEventArgs e)
    {
        LayoutRoot.DataContext = emp;
    }

    private void xChange_Click_1( object sender, RoutedEventArgs e )
    {
        emp.Name = "John";
    }
}
```

When the Employee is created, the name is set to George and the title to President, which is reflected in the UI. When the button is pushed, it simulates a change to the underlying data by changing the name to John. The UI is updated because the Employee class implements INotifyPropertyChanged.

> ■ **Note** In the calls to RaisePropertyChanged, the name of the property being changed is not passed in. Yet the method is able to create the PropertyChangedEventArgs with the calling method's name. This is due to the attribute [CallerMemberName], which sets the caller argument to the name of the calling method. Most of the time this is just what you want, but if you need to override the value, you can pass in a text string that will be used instead.

Binding to Other Elements

Earlier I said that the source for data binding can be any CLR object. This includes UIElements themselves. It is possible (and common!) to bind one UIElement to a value in another. For example, you might bind the IsActive property of a ProgressRing to the IsChecked property of a checkbox, as shown in the next example.

> ■ **Note** A ProgressRing is used to show that work is being done when it is not known how long that work will take.

```
<StackPanel>
    <StackPanel
        Orientation="Horizontal"
        HorizontalAlignment="Left"
        >
        <TextBlock
            Text="ProgressRing:"
            VerticalAlignment="Center"
            Margin="0,0,20,0" />
        <Border
            BorderThickness="1"
            BorderBrush="#44000000"
            Padding="10">
            <ProgressRing
                x:Name="ProgressRing1"
                IsActive="{Binding IsChecked, ElementName=ActiveCB}" />
        </Border>
    </StackPanel>
    <CheckBox
        Name="ActiveCB"
        Content="Active?" />
</StackPanel>
```

Notice that this example has no codebehind. The ProgressRing is active or not depending on the value of its IsActive property. That property is bound to the IsChecked property of the CheckBox. When you check the CheckBox, the ProgressRing becomes active.

Binding and Data Conversion

At times the data in your business object (the source for your binding) and the target UIElement may not have an exact type match. For example, if your Employee class wants to keep track of the start date for each employee, a sensible way to do so is with a DateTime object. However, when you display that data, you want to use a Text object, and you may not want the entire default conversion of a DateTime to a string. To rectify this problem, you can create a class that performs a conversion from one type to another (in this case, from DateTime to string). This class will implement IValueConverter and will have two methods: Convert and ConvertBack. In the following code, you modify the Employee class to add the startDate:

```
private DateTime _startDate;
public DateTime StartDate
{
    get { return _startDate; }
    set { _startDate = value; RaisePropertyChanged(); }
}
```

You then add a new converter class.

```
public class DateConverter : IValueConverter
 {
     public object Convert( object value, Type targetType, object parameter, string language )
     {
         DateTime date = (DateTime)value;
         return date.ToString("d");
     }

     public object ConvertBack( object value, Type targetType, object parameter, string language
)
     {
         string strValue = value as string;
         DateTime resultDateTime;
         if ( DateTime.TryParse( strValue, out resultDateTime ) )
         {
             return resultDateTime;
         }
         throw new Exception( "Unable to convert string to date time" );
     }
 }
```

■ **Note**   Notice the new use of formatting in date.ToString. See http://msdn.microsoft.com/en-us/library/zdtaw1bw.aspx.

You can now create a resource for this class in the XAML. Resources are reusable chunks of code. In this case, since this is a Page.Resource, the code is reusable anywhere in this page. Place the following section below the page declaration but before the declaration of the grid:

```
<Page.Resources>
    <local:DateConverter
        x:Key="DateToStringConverter" />
</Page.Resources>
```

Then you use that resource when you bind to the StartDate.

```
<StackPanel
    Orientation="Horizontal"
    Margin="0,5,0,0">
    <TextBlock
        Text="Start Date" />
    <TextBlock
        Margin="5,0,0,0"
        Height="50"
        Width="200"
        Text="{Binding StartDate, Converter={StaticResource DateToStringConverter } }" />
</StackPanel>
```

As a result, the StartDate property is a DateTime object in the Employee object, but it is represented as a short string in the UI.

Binding to Lists

Often, rather than binding to a single object, you will want to bind to a collection of objects. There are a number of controls for handling collections, and you will examine them in coming chapters. For now, let's focus on how the binding will work.

The trick is to teach the control how to display the bound data. You do this most often with a DataTemplate, a template or set of XAML that will be reproduced for each member of the collection. In the following code, you create a slightly modified Employee class. Each Employee has two properties, Name and Title. You also give the class a static method that returns a list of employees, simulating retrieving data from a web service or other data source.

```
class Employee : INotifyPropertyChanged
    {
        private string _name;
        public string Name
        {
            get { return _name; }
            set
            {
                _name = value;
                RaisePropertyChanged();
            }
        }

        private string _title;
        public string Title
        {
            get { return _title; }
            set
```

```
        {
            _title = value;
            RaisePropertyChanged();
        }
    }

    private void RaisePropertyChanged(
        [CallerMemberName] string caller = "" )
    {
        if ( PropertyChanged != null )
        {
            PropertyChanged( this, new PropertyChangedEventArgs( caller ) );
        }
    }

    public event PropertyChangedEventHandler PropertyChanged;

    public static ObservableCollection<Employee> GetEmployees()
    {
        var employees = new ObservableCollection<Employee>();
        employees.Add( new Employee() { Name = "Washington", Title = "President 1" } );
        employees.Add( new Employee() { Name = "Adams", Title = "President 2" } );
        employees.Add( new Employee() { Name = "Jefferson", Title = "President 3" } );
        employees.Add( new Employee() { Name = "Madison", Title = "President 4" } );
        employees.Add( new Employee() { Name = "Monroe", Title = "President 5" } );
        return employees;
    }

}
```

Notice that the collection type you use for Employee is an ObservableCollection. This type implements INotifyPropertyChanged and INotifyCollectionChanged, and so will inform the UI that the collection has changed. Note that to ensure notification if an individual element in the collection is changed (e.g., an employee's name changes), you must also implement INotifyPropertyChanged on the element type itself.

All you need now is to bind this collection of employees to a control that handles collections of data, such as a ComboBox. The ComboBox has no way of knowing, however, how to display an Employee. Left to its own devices, it will just display whatever ToString resolves to. You *could* override ToString, but it is much more efficient and flexible to teach the ComboBox how to display the Employee exactly as you want, and you do that with a DataTemplate, as shown in the following code:

```
<ComboBox
    x:Name="ComboBox1"
    ItemsSource="{Binding}"
    Foreground="Black"
    FontSize="30"
    Height="50"
    Width="550">
<ComboBox.ItemTemplate>
    <DataTemplate>
        <StackPanel
            Orientation="Horizontal"
```

```
                        Margin="2">
                        <TextBlock
                            Text="Name:"
                            Margin="2" />
                        <TextBlock
                            Text="{Binding Name}"
                            Margin="2" />
                        <TextBlock
                            Text="Title:"
                            Margin="10,2,0,2" />
                        <TextBlock
                            Text="{Binding Title}"
                            Margin="2" />
                    </StackPanel>
                </DataTemplate>
            </ComboBox.ItemTemplate>
        </ComboBox>
```

The ItemTemplate controls how each item is displayed and the DataTemplate lays out how the data is displayed. In this case, you are displaying the data by laying out four TextBlocks horizontally so that each Employee appears on a single line in the ComboBox. Notice that you bind to the ItemsSource property with the keyword binding but you don't specify what you're binding to. This is done by setting the DataContext in the codebehind.

```
protected override void OnNavigatedTo(NavigationEventArgs e)
{
    ComboBox1.ItemsSource = Employee.GetEmployees();
}
```

You set this in the codebehind because you are mimicking the action of retrieving the resource (Employees) from a database or other service. The result is that when the ComboBox is opened, all the Employee objects are displayed, each according to the DataTemplate, as seen in Figure 2-1.

Figure 2-1. ComboBox with DataTemplate and binding

■ **Note** President Kennedy was entertaining a roomful of Nobel Prize winners when he said, "I think this is the most extraordinary collection of talent, of human knowledge, that has ever been gathered at the White House—with the possible exception of when Thomas Jefferson dined alone."

CHAPTER 3

■ ■ ■

Panels

All classes that derive from the Panel abstract base class are referred to as panels. Panels hold other controls and assist in their layout and presentation. Each XAML panel can hold any number of controls in its Children collection. What differentiates the various panels is how it arranges those children.

Canvas, StackPanel, Grid, and VariableSizedWrapGrid all derive directly from Panel as does VirtualizingPanel. OrientedVirtualizingPanel derives from VirtualizingPanel and itself has two derived classes: VirtualizingStackPanel and WrapGrid, as shown in Figure 3-1.

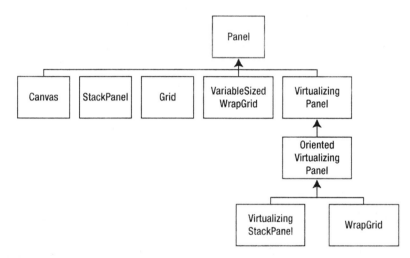

Figure 3-1. Class hierarchy

The most popular panels are Canvas, StackPanel, Grid, and WrapGrid, and so those are the panels I'll focus on for this chapter. You can learn more about the other, less popular panels at http://msdn.microsoft.com/en-us/library/windows/apps/windows.ui.xaml.controls.panel.aspx.

Canvas

The simplest panel is the Canvas. The Canvas uses absolute positioning to layout its elements. Elements use attached properties of Canvas.Left and Canvas.Top to set the offset from the upper left hand corner of the Canvas. Canvas also uses Canvas.ZIndex to define the apparent ordering of elements one on top of another.

> ■ **Note** Attached properties are not part of the class that uses them; they are part of another class. Thus, none of the controls such as button have a Canvas.Left or even a Left property; they attach this property from the Canvas class.

Each element is considered to be enclosed by a rectangle, the upper left hand corner of which is placed at the left/top coordinates you specify. The following code illustrates creating a number of elements and placing them on the canvas:

> ■ **Note** Place this code between the opening and closing <Page> tags in MainPage.xaml.

```
<Canvas>
    <TextBlock
        Text="Hello World!!"
        Canvas.Top="40"
        Canvas.Left="40" />
    <Rectangle
        Fill="Red"
        Height="50"
        Width="70"
        Canvas.Top="80"
        Canvas.Left="40" />
    <Ellipse
        Fill="Yellow"
        Height="75"
        Width="75"
        Canvas.Top="40"
        Canvas.Left="150" />
</Canvas>
```

This creates three objects, each offset by the designated amount from the top left corner, as shown in Figure 3-2.

> ■ **Note** This and subsequent illustrations assume that the page color is black, which you can set in the Page element, like <Page Background="Black" …>.

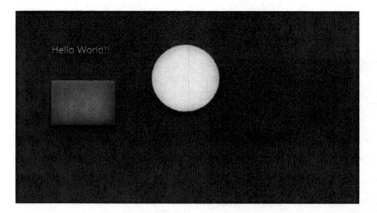

Figure 3-2. Three objects

It is possible for the objects to overlap. In that case, the objects created later will overlap on top of the objects created earlier, unless you specify a z-order, as shown in the following code:

```
<Canvas>
    <Rectangle
        Height="50"
        Width="70"
        Canvas.Left="40"
        Canvas.Top="40"
        Fill="Red" />

    <Rectangle
        Height="50"
        Width="70"
        Canvas.Left="75"
        Canvas.Top="50"
        Fill="Blue" />
    <Rectangle
        Height="50"
        Width="70"
        Canvas.Left="110"
        Canvas.Top="60"
        Canvas.ZIndex="10"
        Fill="Red" />

    <Rectangle
        Height="50"
        Width="70"
        Canvas.Left="145"
        Canvas.Top="70"
        Fill="Blue" />
</Canvas>
```

Here you have four overlapping rectangles, placed onto the canvas in the order Red-Blue-Red-Blue. That is how they would display, except that the default z-order is zero and the third rectangle has a declared z-order of 10, as set by the ZIndex property. This pushes the third rectangle out on top of the others, as shown in Figure 3-3.

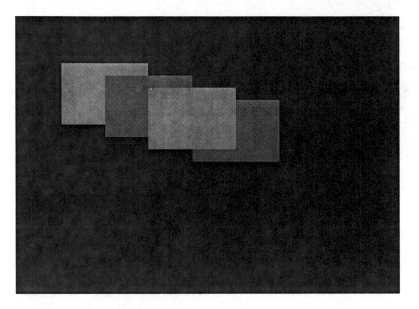

Figure 3-3. Three rectangles

Stack Panel

You saw the StackPanel in Chapter 1. It allows you to place objects either one on top of another, or one to the side of another. There are no attached properties to set; the stack panel handles the layout itself.

StackPanels are popular in Windows 8 programming because they are adaptable to the screen size. Each object is given the room it needs in the panel, and the panel itself can be set to stretch to the available room. Items are placed right next to one another by default, so it is common to set margins to allow for a bit of spacing. Let's take a look at stacking items in the following code:

```
<StackPanel
    Name="LayoutRoot"
    VerticalAlignment="Stretch">
    <TextBlock
        Text="Red Rectangle"
        Margin="5"
        FontSize="40"/>
    <Rectangle
        Height="40"
        Width="60"
        Fill="Red"
        Margin="5"
        HorizontalAlignment="Left"/>
    <StackPanel
        Name="InnerStack"
        Orientation="Horizontal">
```

```
        <TextBlock
            Text="Blue Rectangle"
            FontSize="40"
            Margin="5" />
        <Rectangle
            Height="40"
            Width="60"
            Fill="Blue"
            Margin="5" />

    </StackPanel>
</StackPanel>
```

The outer StackPanel's orientation is vertical (the default) and so the red rectangle is placed below the TextBlock. The inner StackPanel is placed below that, but since its orientation has been set to horizontal, its contents (the TextBlock and the blue rectangle) are placed next to one another, as shown in Figure 3-4.

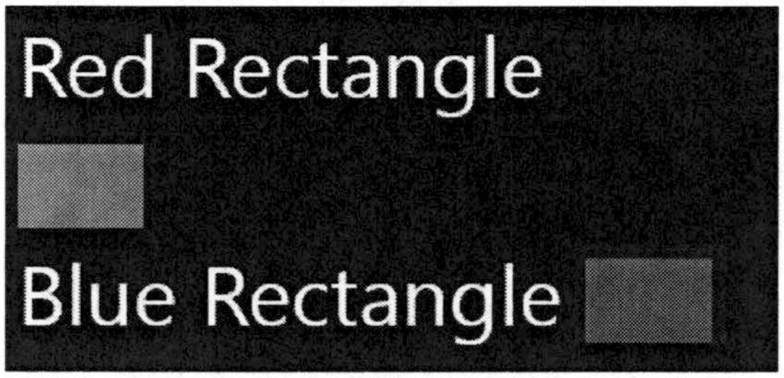

Figure 3-4. Red and blue rectangle

Grid

The Grid is by far the most popular of the panels. It is the most flexible and makes placement of controls on the page easy. More importantly in Windows 8, the Grid will allow your controls to expand or contract based on the available space. Given that Windows 8 applications must run on everything from small slate computers to giant desktop monitors, this can be critically important.

The Grid is so popular that it is the default panel created for you when you start a new application or create a new page. A grid consists of rows and columns. You can specify the number and size of both rows and columns, and you can specify the size in any of three ways:

- Explicit size (e.g., 20px)

- Automatic size

- Relative size

Explicit size is the easiest to understand but the least useful much of the time. When you specify that a row will be 50px high, it will be exactly that—no higher and no less high. When you use automatic sizing, the row will be as high as the tallest control you place in the row and the column will be as wide as the widest control it holds. Relative sizing, sometimes called start sizing, asks Windows to take all the remaining size (after allocating for explicit and automatic size) and divides it up among all the relative sized rows (or columns) proportionally. To see how this works, let's declare a few rows.

```
<Grid.RowDefinitions>
    <RowDefinition
        Height="80" />
    <RowDefinition
        Height="Auto" />
    <RowDefinition
        Height="Auto" />
    <RowDefinition
        Height="4*" />
    <RowDefinition
        Height="2*" />
    <RowDefinition
        Height="*" />
</Grid.RowDefinitions>
```

The first row is defined to have a height of 80 pixels. It will have that height no matter what you place in the row. The second and third rows are marked with a height of Auto and will size themselves based on what is placed in the rows. The final three rows use relative (or star) sizing.

The first of these is 4* and the second is 2*, so the first will be twice as large as the second. The third just has a star with no number, which is equivalent to 1*, so the second will be twice as big as this. Another way to think about this is that there is a total of 7*, so the remaining space (after the 80 and the two Auto rows) will be divided into sevenths, with the first of the relative rows receiving 4/7 of the space, the second receiving 2/7, and the final row receiving 1/7.

Now let's add rectangles to the grid.

```
<Rectangle Fill="Red"
           VerticalAlignment="Top"
           Grid.Row="0"
           Height="50"
           Width="50" />
<Rectangle Fill="Red"
           VerticalAlignment="Top"
           Grid.Row="1"
           Height="50"
           Width="50" />
<Rectangle Fill="Red"
           VerticalAlignment="Top"
           Grid.Row="2"
           Height="50"
           Width="50" />
<Rectangle Fill="Red"
           VerticalAlignment="Top"
           Grid.Row="3"
           Height="50"
           Width="50" />
<Rectangle Fill="Red"
           VerticalAlignment="Top"
           Grid.Row="4"
           Height="50"
           Width="50" />
<Rectangle Fill="Red"
```

```
VerticalAlignment="Top"
Grid.Row="5"
Height="50"
Width="50" />
```

Let's take a look at the output, shown in Figure 3-5, and see if we can make sense of it.

Figure 3-5. Placing rectangles

The first rectangle is 50 units high and the row is 80, so you see a margin at the bottom of 30 units. Note that all the rectangles were set with VerticalAlignment = top, meaning they will cling to the top of their row. The next three are all together with no space between them. This is because two of the next three are autosized and thus fill their space, and the third of the three is the first of the relative sized rows and the rectangle is at the very top of that row. You can see that it gets twice as much space as the one below it, which in turn has twice as much space as the final rectangle.

WrapGrid

With a normal Grid you specify the number of rows and columns and then populate the resulting cells with controls. With a WrapGrid you supply a collection of objects to the wrap grid and it lays them out in columns, wrapping to the next row as required (or, conversely, it lays them out in rows, wrapping to the next column as needed).

The WrapGrid itself must be inside an items control, as shown in the following code:

```
<ItemsControl
    x:Name="xItems">
    <ItemsControl.ItemsPanel>
        <ItemsPanelTemplate>
            <WrapGrid Orientation="Horizontal" />
        </ItemsPanelTemplate>
    </ItemsControl.ItemsPanel>
 </ItemsControl>
```

The ItemsControl wraps an ItemsPanel which in turn has an ItemsPanelTemplate. Inside the template you place your WrapGrid, in this case adding the attribute orientation = "Horizontal" so that the items will lay out in rows rather than in columns.

The codebehind populates the WrapGrid by adding controls to it, and the grid takes care of laying out the controls depending on the available room. In this example, just to show that it can be done, you'll add the TextBlocks programmatically. Not only is that wicked cool, but it saves adding 200 TextBlocks by hand to the XAML.

```
protected override void OnNavigatedTo(NavigationEventArgs e)
{
    for ( int i = 0; i < 200; i++ )
    {
        xItems.Items.Add( new TextBlock() { Text = "hello", Margin=new Thickness(20) } );
    }
}
```

When you run out of room in one row, the WrapGrid wraps the next control to the second row, and so forth, as shown in Figure 3-6.

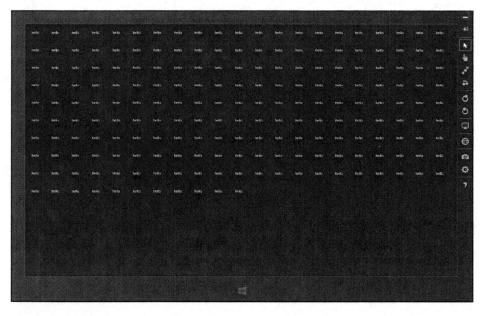

Figure 3-6. WrapGrid

Border

Border does not inherit from Panel, but it is often used as a panel, so I've included here because it is a popular control. While there are other creative uses for Border, its principle usage is to create a border around one or more controls (hence the name). When you create a border, you define the border color and the thickness of the border. You might also define the size of the border and its alignment, especially if it is going to sit inside a slot bigger than the border itself (e.g., inside a grid with one cell). This is illustrated in the following code:

```
<Border
    BorderBrush="Blue"
    BorderThickness="3"
    Width="200"
    Height="100"
    HorizontalAlignment="Left"
    VerticalAlignment="Top"
    Margin="20">
    <TextBlock
        Text="I'm inside a border!" />
</Border>
```

CHAPTER 4

■ ■ ■

Controls

The heart and soul of Windows 8 programming is embodied in the controls available to you in the Toolbox.
I'll show you the most important controls and how to use them in your application. The goal is not to
provide a comprehensive reference guide but rather to illustrate how to declare these controls in the XAML
and obtain a lot of flexibility with a minimum of coding.

TextControls

You've already seen the work-horse controls for text, TextBlock and TextBox, in Chapter 1. One notable
aspect of the Text controls is that rather than having a Content property (which can be just about anything)
they have a Text property as they are optimized for the display and manipulation of text (see the "Content"
sidebar). A common use of TextBlock is as a label, and of course TextBoxes are used to gather input from
the user.

CONTENT

Many controls have a Content property. Much of the time the Content property is populated with a simple
string, but that need not be so. Content can hold text or any UIElement, but it can only hold one. Thus, the
most common element to put into Content (after text) is a panel, which in turn can hold any number of
elements. If you want a button, for example, with three lines of text, you assign a panel to the Button's
Content property, and then three TextBlocks to the panel. The resulting code might look like this:

```
<Button Name="ContentButton">

    <StackPanel>

        <TextBlock

            Text="First line of text" />

        <TextBlock

            Text="Second line of text" />

        <TextBlock

            Text="Third line of text" />
```

```
    </StackPanel>

  </Button>
```

The result is shown in Figure 4-1.

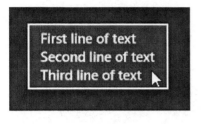

Figure 4-1. *Three lines of text in a button*

PasswordBox

PasswordBox is very much like TextBox except that the characters typed into the box are masked (hidden from view) for purposes of keeping them secret. The default masking character is a bullet (·) but you can change that to any character you like using the PasswordCharproperty. You can also determine if there will be a "reveal" button in the text box that, when held, shows the password in clear text, as shown in Figure 4-2.

????????

Figure 4-2. *Reveal button*

The following code illustrates both changing the default masking character and setting the IsPasswordRevealButtonEnabled to true:

```
<StackPanel
    VerticalAlignment="Top"
    HorizontalAlignment="Left">
    <PasswordBox
        PasswordChar="?"
        IsPasswordRevealButtonEnabled="True"
        Name="xPassword"
        Width="200"
        Height="50"
        LostFocus="xPassword_LostFocus_1" />
    <TextBox
        Name="Dummy"
        Width="200"
        Height="50"
        Margin="20" />
    <TextBlock
```

```
        Margin="20"
        Name="Message"
        Text="Ready..." />
</StackPanel>
```

This codebehind supports the LostFocus event, which is fired when the PasswordBox loses focus (e.g., the user tabs to another control).

```
private void xPassword_LostFocus_1( object sender, RoutedEventArgs e )
{
    Message.Text = xPassword.Password;
}
```

RichEditBox

The RichEditBox allows the user to open and view and edit a Rich Text Format (RTF) document. "Rich text" refers to all the text attributes you associate with a word processor but not with a text editor (e.g., bold, color, etc.). The RichEditBox control handles all the work of understanding and presenting the rich text. The following code illustrates creating and using a RichEditBox control:

```
<Grid
    Margin="120">
    <Grid.RowDefinitions>
        <RowDefinition
            Height="50" />
        <RowDefinition />
    </Grid.RowDefinitions>
    <Button
        Content="Open file"
        Click="Button_Click_1" />
    <RichEditBox
        Name="editor"
        Grid.Row="1" />
</Grid>
```

The codebehind to support the RichEditBox is shown here and explained in detail below:

```
private async void Button_Click_1( object sender, RoutedEventArgs e )
{
    Windows.Storage.Pickers.FileOpenPicker open =
        new Windows.Storage.Pickers.FileOpenPicker();
    open.SuggestedStartLocation =
        Windows.Storage.Pickers.PickerLocationId.DocumentsLibrary;
    open.FileTypeFilter.Add( ".rtf" );
    open.FileTypeFilter.Add( ".txt" );

    Windows.Storage.StorageFile file = await open.PickSingleFileAsync();

    Windows.Storage.Streams.IRandomAccessStream randAccStream =
        await file.OpenAsync( Windows.Storage.FileAccessMode.Read );

    editor.Document.LoadFromStream(
```

```
            Windows.UI.Text.TextSetOptions.FormatRtf, randAccStream );
}
```

In this code, an instance of `FileOpenPicker` is created and named open. The start location (where to start looking for documents) is set to the Documents library, and the file types to open are set as rtf and txt. An instance of `StorageFile` named file is then created by calling `PickSingleFileAsync()` on open. This opens the file picker, as seen in Figure 4-3.

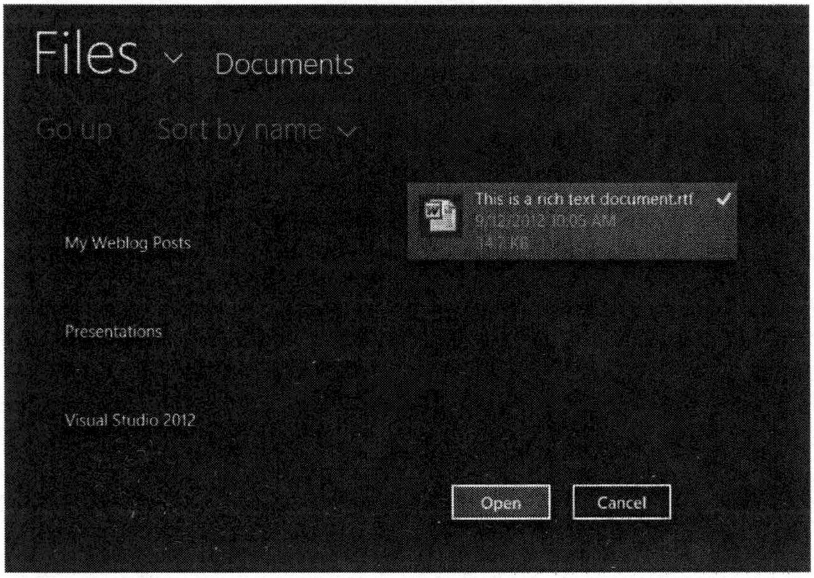

Figure 4-3. A file picker

The `await` keyword causes the method to wait for the results before continuing. For more on the await keyword, please see the "Await" sidebar.

An instance of the interface `IRandomAccessStream` is created by calling `OpenAsync` on file, passing in that you want the file to be opened in read-only mode. With the stream in hand, you load the document into your `RichEditBox`, passing in the format you want to use (rtf) and the access stream. The file is read into the `RichEditBox`, as shown in Figure 4-4.

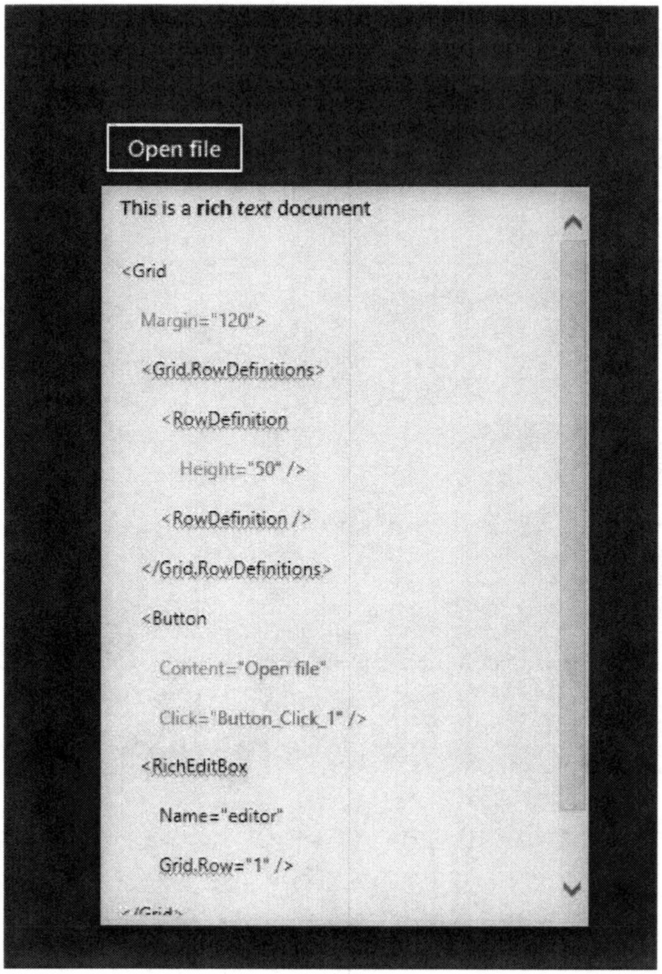

Open file

This is a **rich** *text* document

```
<Grid

  Margin="120">

  <Grid.RowDefinitions>

    <RowDefinition

      Height="50" />

    <RowDefinition />

  </Grid.RowDefinitions>

  <Button

    Content="Open file"

    Click="Button_Click_1" />

  <RichEditBox

    Name="editor"

    Grid.Row="1" />

  </Grid>
```

Figure 4-4. RichEditBox XAML

Selection Controls

The next sections will cover the various selection controls.

Button, ToggleButton, HyperlinkButton

The classic Button looks and feels like a real-life button. You push it and it appears to depress. More importantly, when you push it, something happens (the elevator comes, the light comes on, nuclear war commences…). In XAML programming, you designate what is to happen by assigning a handler to one or more events. The most common event for Button is Click. You write the code for what is to happen when the Click button is raised in the Click button event handler. A ToggleButton is much like a regular button except that it toggles between two states and reflects which state it is in (on/off) in its appearance. Finally, a HyperlinkButton acts like a button but also navigates to a new location (typically a new page in your application). The following code illustrates these three button types:

```
<StackPanel Margin="20">
    <Button
        Name="xButton"
        Content="Standard Button"
        Click="xButton_Click_1" />
    <ToggleButton
        Name="xToggleButton"
        Content="ToggleButton"
        Checked="xToggleButton_Checked_1"
        Unchecked="xToggleButton_Unchecked_1"/>
    <HyperlinkButton
        Name="xHyperlinkButton"
        Content="HyperLinkButton"
        NavigateUri="http://JesseLiberty.com"
        Click="xHyperlinkButton_Click_1"/>
    <TextBlock
        Name="Message"
        Text="Ready..." />
</StackPanel>
```

Notice that each of the buttons has an event and a named event handler, shown in bold. In fact, ToggleButton has two events (Checked and Unchecked). These event handlers are written in the codebehind file, as shown:

```
private void xButton_Click_1( object sender, RoutedEventArgs e )
{
    Message.Text = "Regular button clicked!";
}


private void xToggleButton_Checked_1( object sender, RoutedEventArgs e )
{
    Message.Text = "Toggle button is \"on\"";
}

private void xToggleButton_Unchecked_1( object sender, RoutedEventArgs e )
{
    Message.Text = "Toggle button is \"off\"";

}

private void xHyperlinkButton_Click_1( object sender, RoutedEventArgs e )
{
    Message.Text = "Hyperlink was clicked!";
}
```

▪ **Note** The HyperLinkButton not only has an event, but also causes navigation via the NavigateUri property in the XAML.

Content for Controls

As will be true most of the time, the content for the buttons shown above was just text. You can, however, assign any content you like because buttons are content controls and the Content property does not have to take just a string. You can add virtually any content you like to a button, such as a shape (see below) or a pane that then contains multiple controls, as illustrated in the following code and shown in Figure 4-5:

```
<StackPanel>
    <Button Content="This button has text" />
    <Button>
        <Rectangle
            Height="30"
            Width="60"
            Fill="Red" />
    </Button>
    <Button>
        <StackPanel>
            <Ellipse
                Height="40"
                Width="40"
                Fill="Red" />
            <TextBlock>Push Me!</TextBlock>
        </StackPanel>
    </Button>
</StackPanel>
```

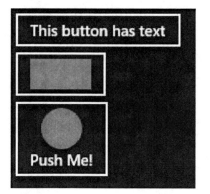

Figure 4-5. Push me!

CheckBox

CheckBox controls are not as common in Windows 8 as they were in previous versions of Windows, as they have been more or less supplanted by ToggleButtons (see below). That said, they still have their purpose, allowing either for the user to choose one of two states (yes/no) or three states (yes/no/indeterminate). To see this at work, create a new project and add the XAML and codebehind shown here:

```xml
<StackPanel Margin="20">
<CheckBox
    Name="xCheckBox"
    VerticalAlignment="Top"
    HorizontalAlignment="Left"
    Content="Loves XAML"
    Checked="xCheckBox_Checked_1"
    Unchecked="xCheckBox_Unchecked_1"
    IsThreeState="True"
    Indeterminate="xCheckBox_Indeterminate_1" />

    <TextBlock
        Name="Message"
        Text="Ready..."
        VerticalAlignment="Top"
        HorizontalAlignment="Left" />
</StackPanel>
```

```csharp
private void xCheckBox_Checked_1( object sender, RoutedEventArgs e )
{
    Message.Text = "You DO love XAML, I knew it.";
}

private void xCheckBox_Unchecked_1( object sender, RoutedEventArgs e )
{
    Message.Text = "Hang in there, it gets better.";
}

private void xCheckBox_Indeterminate_1( object sender, RoutedEventArgs e )
{
    Message.Text = "Some people can't make up their mind.";
}
```

The checked checkbox has an x in it, the unchecked check box is empty, and the indeterminate has a square in it, as shown in Figure 4-6.

Figure 4-6. A checkbox and some text

ToggleSwitch

ToggleSwitch is a very intuitive way of asking the user to choose one of two states. As such, it has come close to replacing the CheckBox. When you create a ToggleSwitch control, you provide text for the header for the content when the switch is on and the content for when it is off. The on and off content replace one another when the switch is toggled. Here's some simple XAML to create a toggle switch (no codebehind is needed unless you want to react to the change in state):

```
<ToggleSwitch
    Header="Having fun yet?"
    OnContent="Yup"
    OffContent="Nope"
    Width="130" />
```

The result of adding this code and toggling the switch on is shown in Figure 4-7.

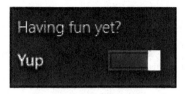

Figure 4-7. *Toggle switch in action*

RadioButton

RadioButtons allow for the setting of two or more mutually exclusive choices. In the following code, you see two sets (groups) of RadioButtons. One asks the user to choose among two alternatives (true/false) and the second group asks the user to choose among three alternatives. In both cases, only one choice can be made at a time (when you click one radio button, the currently selected button is de-selected).

▦ **Note**   Radio buttons are named and modeled after the old-fashioned radio buttons from automobiles, where you would physically push one button in and the currently chosen button would pop out, thus allowing you to select one station at a time. This is back from the days when there were no computers, roads were unpaved, and horses ran wild through the streets.

```
<StackPanel>
    <StackPanel
        Orientation="Horizontal">
        <RadioButton
            Name="xRB1"
            GroupName="Truth"
            Content="True"
            IsChecked="True" />
        <RadioButton
            Margin="5,0,0,0"
            Name="xRB2"
            GroupName="Truth"
```

45

```
            Content="False" />
    </StackPanel>
    <StackPanel
        Orientation="Horizontal">
        <RadioButton
            Name="xRB3"
            GroupName="Quality"
            Content="Excellent"
            IsChecked="True" />
        <RadioButton
            Margin="5,0,0,0"
            Name="xRB4"
            GroupName="Quality"
            Content="Good" />
        <RadioButton
            Margin="5,0,0,0"
            Name="xRB5"
            GroupName="Quality"
            Content="Poor" />
    </StackPanel>
</StackPanel>
```

No codebehind is needed unless you wish to be notified when a button is clicked or when a button is checked or unchecked, in which case you would use the respective event handlers.

ListView and GridView

The ListView and GridView both display collections of data. They both derive from ItemsControl and have very similar functionality, but their appearance is quite different.

The ListView stacks items vertically. The GridView puts items into a grid (hence the name) and effectively stacks them horizontally and then vertically. The ListView takes up relatively little room and is often used in snapped view. The GridView is a richer control and is used when each item needs more space, such as with a photo gallery.

Either ItemsControl can be populated directly either in XAML or in code, or can be populated through data binding using the ItemsSource property. Because they are best suited to different views, it is common to have both a ListView and a GridView bound to the same data, allowing you to make visible whichever control is appropriate.

To add items directly to a ListView using XAML just add them within the element, as shown here:

```
<ListView
    Name="xListView"
    <x:String>Item 1</x:String>
    <x:String>Item 2</x:String>
    <x:String>Item 3</x:String>
</ListView>
```

You can generate the items in code just as easily, adding them to the Items collection of the ItemsControl.

```
protected override void OnNavigatedTo(NavigationEventArgs e)
{
    GridView xGridView = new GridView();
```

```
    xGridView.Items.Add( "Item 1" );
    xGridView.Items.Add( "Item 2" );
    xGridView.Items.Add( "Item 3" );
    xStackPanel.Children.Add( xGridView );
}
```

Items added to an `ItemsControl` are wrapped in an item container, `ListViewItem` or `GridViewItem`, respectively. If you wish to change the display of the item, you can apply a style to the item container by way of the `ItemContainerStyle` property, as you'll see in the Chapter 5.

Note that when you added items programmatically, you explicitly added them to the `Items` collection. Items added via XAML are added to the `Items` collection automatically. Thus this code

```
<ListView
    Name="xListView"
    <x:String>Item 1</x:String>
    <x:String>Item 2</x:String>
    <x:String>Item 3</x:String>
</ListView>
```

is really the same as writing

```
<ListView
    Name="xListView"
 <ListView.Items>
    <x:String>Item 1</x:String>
    <x:String>Item 2</x:String>
    <x:String>Item 3</x:String>
  </ListView.Items>
</ListView>
```

It is more common to add items to an `ItemsControl` from a collection, typically retrieved from a web service or a database, and to use data binding. To populate an `ItemsControl` in this way, you set its `ItemsSource` property to your collection of data, much as you did in the example with the `ComboBox`. Similarly to that example, you may choose to create a `DataTemplate` to control how the list is shown, in either the `ListView` or the `GridView`.

AppBar

Windows-style applications focus on content, not chrome. Part of traditional chrome is buttons used for command and navigation. How do you provide this functionality to the user without adding chrome back into the application? The answer is to put the command and navigation buttons into an app bar that slides up from the bottom (or down from the top) on request, as shown in Figure 4-8.

Figure 4-8. The app bar showing at bottom of application

The app bar is brought into view by sliding up from the bottom (or down from the top) of the screen. It has an IsSticky attribute. If that attribute is set to true, then you dismiss the app bar with the same gesture that brought it into view. If IsSticky is false, then you can tap anywhere on the application (outside of the app bar itself) to dismiss the app bar.

The StandardStyles.xaml file, which is added under the Common folder when you create your application, has a number of button images that you can use in the app bar, as shown in Figure 4-8 and in the following code:

```xml
    <Style x:Key="SaveAppBarButtonStyle" TargetType="Button" BasedOn="{StaticResource
AppBarButtonStyle}">
        <Setter Property="AutomationProperties.AutomationId" Value="SaveAppBarButton"/>
        <Setter Property="AutomationProperties.Name" Value="Save"/>
        <Setter Property="Content" Value="&#xE105;"/>
    </Style>
    <Style x:Key="DeleteAppBarButtonStyle" TargetType="Button" BasedOn="{StaticResource
AppBarButtonStyle}">
        <Setter Property="AutomationProperties.AutomationId" Value="DeleteAppBarButton"/>
        <Setter Property="AutomationProperties.Name" Value="Delete"/>
        <Setter Property="Content" Value="&#xE106;"/>
    </Style>
    <Style x:Key="DiscardAppBarButtonStyle" TargetType="Button" BasedOn="{StaticResource
AppBarButtonStyle}">
        <Setter Property="AutomationProperties.AutomationId" Value="DiscardAppBarButton"/>
        <Setter Property="AutomationProperties.Name" Value="Discard"/>
        <Setter Property="Content" Value="&#xE107;"/>
    </Style>
    <Style x:Key="RemoveAppBarButtonStyle" TargetType="Button" BasedOn="{StaticResource
AppBarButtonStyle}">
        <Setter Property="AutomationProperties.AutomationId" Value="RemoveAppBarButton"/>
        <Setter Property="AutomationProperties.Name" Value="Remove"/>
        <Setter Property="Content" Value="&#xE108;"/>
    </Style>
    <Style x:Key="AddAppBarButtonStyle" TargetType="Button" BasedOn="{StaticResource
AppBarButtonStyle}">
        <Setter Property="AutomationProperties.AutomationId" Value="AddAppBarButton"/>
        <Setter Property="AutomationProperties.Name" Value="Add"/>
```

```
        <Setter Property="Content" Value="&#xE109;"/>
    </Style>
```

Styles are covered in detail in Chapter 5; however you can see here that these styles, when applied to a button, will add the glyph and behavior expected for the button. To create the app bar itself, declare the AppBar class at the page level, as shown here:

```
<Page.BottomAppBar>
    <AppBar
        x:Name="BottomAppBar1"
        Padding="10,0,10,0">
        <Grid>
            <Grid.ColumnDefinitions>
                <ColumnDefinition
                    Width="50*" />
                <ColumnDefinition
                    Width="50*" />
            </Grid.ColumnDefinitions>
            <StackPanel
                x:Name="LeftPanel"
                Orientation="Horizontal"
                Grid.Column="0"
                HorizontalAlignment="Left">
                <Button
                    x:Name="Edit"
                    Style="{StaticResource EditAppBarButtonStyle}"
                    Click="AppBarButtonClick"
                    Tag="Edit" />
                <Button
                    x:Name="Save"
                    Click="AppBarButtonClick"
                    Style="{StaticResource SaveAppBarButtonStyle}"
                    Tag="Save" />
                <Button
                    x:Name="Remove"
                    Click="AppBarButtonClick"
                    Style="{StaticResource RemoveAppBarButtonStyle}"
                    Tag="Delete" />
            </StackPanel>
            <StackPanel
                x:Name="RightPanel"
                Orientation="Horizontal"
                Grid.Column="1"
                HorizontalAlignment="Right">
                <Button
                    x:Name="Refresh"
                    Click="AppBarButtonClick"
                    Style="{StaticResource RefreshAppBarButtonStyle}"
                    Tag="Refresh" />
                <Button
                    x:Name="Help"
```

```
                    Click="AppBarButtonClick"
                    Style="{StaticResource HelpAppBarButtonStyle}"
                    Tag="Help" />
            </StackPanel>
        </Grid>
    </AppBar>
</Page.BottomAppBar>
```

You start the AppBar by creating a grid with two columns, left and right for the sets of buttons. By convention, application-specific buttons appear on the left, while more global buttons appear on the right. You then align the buttons by using horizontal stack panels, and each button is given a name, a style (for the glyph), and a tag. The tag is used in handling the click event (in this example, all of the buttons share the same click event handler).

The page itself consists of a few controls stacked one atop another.

```
<Grid
    Background="{StaticResource ApplicationPageBackgroundThemeBrush}">
    <StackPanel>
        <TextBlock
            Text="Slide up for the app bar"
            FontSize="50" />
        <ToggleSwitch
            Name="xToggleSwitch1"
            Header="Sticky?"
            OnContent="Yup"
            OffContent="Nope"
            Toggled="ToggleSwitch_Toggled_1" />
        <TextBlock
            Name="xMessage"
            FontSize="40" />
    </StackPanel>
</Grid>
```

The ToggleSwitch toggles between IsSticky mode being on and off. The third control is a TextBlock named xMessage. When a button is clicked, you obtain the tag property of that button and use it to display which button was clicked in the Message TextBlock. Here's the codebehind for the page:

```
private void ToggleSwitch_Toggled_1( object sender, RoutedEventArgs e )
{
        BottomAppBar1.IsSticky = xToggleSwitch1.IsOn;
}

private void AppBarButtonClick( object sender, RoutedEventArgs e )
{
    Button b = e.OriginalSource as Button;
    var t = b.Tag;
    string msg = t.ToString();

    xMessage.Text = String.Format("You clicked {0} !", msg);

}
```

Shapes

XAML has two built in shapes (Ellipse and Rectangle) and the ability to create arbitrary shapes using Paths.

Ellipse and Rectangle

Ellipses and circles, rectangles and squares can all be created in XAML just by declaring an instance and setting the width and height (if the width and height are equal, you will have a circle or square). The shapes can be used in a variety of ways, including in custom creation of buttons and other controls (see Chapter 6 on templates).

The following code creates four shapes and places them onto a Canvas. The result is shown in Figure 4-9.

```
<Canvas>
    <Ellipse
        Width="200"
        Height="100"
        Fill="Red"
        Canvas.Left="20"
        Canvas.Top="20" />
    <Rectangle
        Width="200"
        Height="100"
        Fill="Blue"
        Canvas.Left="300"
        Canvas.Top="20" />
    <Ellipse
        Width="200"
        Height="200"
        Fill="Green"
        Canvas.Left="20"
        Canvas.Top="200" />
    <Rectangle
        Width="200"
        Height="200"
        Fill="Purple"
        Canvas.Left="300"
        Canvas.Top="200" />
</Canvas>
```

■ **Note** In this code, Canvas replaces the outermost grid rather than being placed inside it.

Figure 4-9. Canvas with shapes

Path

You can also draw on the Canvas with a Path, like so:

```
<Path
    Stroke="DarkBlue"
    StrokeThickness="4"
    Data="M 200,100 C 100,50 300,350 500,175 H 280" />
```

The Path statement uses a special encoding. Briefly, M indicates the starting offset (200 on the x axis and 100 down from the top on the y axis). M indicates "move to without drawing." The C indicates a cubic Bezier curve from the starting point (200,100) to its ending point (500,175) using two control points (100,50 and 300,350). A control point is a turning point in the curve—a cubic Bezier has two turning points or bends. The H indicates a horizontal line, which is drawn from where the line happens to be (500,175) to a new endpoint at 280,175. Notice that since the y coordinate in the end point didn't change, it need not be specified. Typically, paths are not created by hand but by a tool such as Expression Blend; see Figure 4-10.

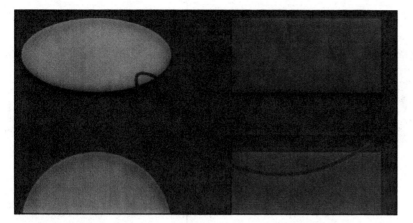

Figure 4-10. *A path on a canvas*

Presentation Controls

There are various presentation controls that are available to you.

Slider

The Slider control provides a visual representation of numeric values or allows the user to select from a range of values by moving the thumb along the slider (see Figure 4-11). In the following code, you bind the value from the Slider to the TextBlock, causing the current value of the slider to appear in the TextBlock.

```
<StackPanel>
    <StackPanel
        Orientation="Horizontal"
        Margin="0,20,0,0">
        <TextBlock
            Text="Slider: " />
        <Slider
            x:Name="xSlider"
            Width="130"
            Margin="60,0,0,0"
            VerticalAlignment="Center" />
    </StackPanel>
    <StackPanel
        Orientation="Horizontal">
        <TextBlock
            Text="Value: " />
        <TextBlock
            x:Name="xSliderValue"
            Text="{Binding Value, ElementName=xSlider}"
            Margin="10,0,0,0" />
    </StackPanel>
</StackPanel>
```

The value in the TextBlock is updated immediately as the slider is moved, as shown in Figure 4-11.

Figure 4-11. Moving the slider and updating the TextBlock

Image

Adding an image to your application is shockingly easy using the Image control. Place the image in a known location (typically an images folder) and add the Image control to your application, providing attributes to determine the height and width of the image you want to display, and how you want the image stretched if it does not match the aspect ratio you specify. The possible stretch values are

- **None**: Preserves the original size
- **Fill:** Resizes to fit dimensions; ignores original aspect ratio
- **Uniform:** Resizes to fit dimensions; preserves original aspect ratio
- **Uniform To Fill:** Resizes to fit dimensions; ignores original aspect ratio; if necessary, clips to fit

The following code illustrates adding an image to a project:

```
<StackPanel
    Orientation="Horizontal"
    Margin="0,20,0,0">
    <TextBlock
        Text="Your Author: " />
    <Image
        x:Name="AuthorImage"
        Source="images/Jesse.jpg"
        Width="400"
        Height="500"
        Stretch="UniformToFill"
        Margin="10,0,0,0" />
</StackPanel>
```

FlipView

The FlipView control allows the user to flip through a sequence of items, one by one. A typical use for the FlipView control would be to make an image browser. In its basic form, it is an incredibly simple and easy control to use. You just tell it where the images are and it takes care of the rest, as shown in the following code:

```
<FlipView Name="xFlipView">
    <Image
        Source="images/Alnwick.jpg" />
    <Image
        Source="images/kings.jpg" />
    <Image
        Source="images/maine.jpg" />
    <Image
        Source="images/peace.jpg" />
 </FlipView>
```

This small block of code is sufficient to display these four images one at a time, allowing the user to move from one to the next with the flick of a finger or the click of a mouse.

If you have more than a handful of images, however, you will want to assign a collection to the FlipView, which you can do through its ItemsSource property. In the following code, you will create a collection of Image objects, and then add your images to that collection before making that collection the ItemsSource for your FlipView. The first image is added one step at a time and the following images do the same work but all in one line.

```
protected override void OnNavigatedTo(NavigationEventArgs e)
{
    var images = new List<Image>();

    var img = new Image();
    img.Source = new BitmapImage( new Uri( this.BaseUri, @"images/alnwick.jpg" ) );
    images.Add( img );

    images.Add( new Image() { Source = new BitmapImage( new Uri( this.BaseUri, @"images/kings.
jpg" ) ) } );
    images.Add( new Image() { Source = new BitmapImage( new Uri( this.BaseUri, @"images/maine.
jpg" ) ) } );
    images.Add( new Image() { Source = new BitmapImage( new Uri( this.BaseUri, @"images/peace.
jpg" ) ) } );
    images.Add( new Image() { Source = new BitmapImage( new Uri( this.BaseUri, @"images/round.
jpg" ) ) } );
    images.Add( new Image() { Source = new BitmapImage( new Uri( this.BaseUri, @"images/sheep.
jpg" ) ) } );


    xFlipView.ItemsSource = images;

}
```

Imagine that instead of hard-coding these paths, you can obtain the images from a database or other server. In any case, once you have the collection, you assign it to the ItemsSource of FlipView and voila! an image carousel.

MediaElement

MediaElement is another one of those controls, like FlipView, that let you create an amazing user experience with virtually no code. You can then go on to add features to your heart's delight, but getting started is wicked simple. In the following code, you declare a MediaElement and point it at a video clip you've placed into a folder named media. That's all you have to do. AutoPlay is set to true so when you run the application the video starts up in full screen mode. Nice.

```
<MediaElement
    Name="xMedia"
    AutoPlay="True"
    Source="media/Wildlife.wmv" />
```

It is worth noting, however, that there is a lot more you can do with MediaElement. You can start out, of course, with adding buttons for stop, pause, resume, etc., but then go on to add markers so that you can provide the user with additional meta-information, or set the style, add special effects, etc. MediaElement supports MPEG-4, MPEG-2, ASF, ADTS, MP-3, WAV, AVI, and AC-3. One could write a book (and not a bad idea) on MediaElement.

Popup

The Popup class provides support for creating popups in your application, but the body of the popup itself is a user control that you create. In the following code, you create a user control as the popup content. The user control consists of a StackPanel with two TextBlocks and a Button.

```
<UserControl
    x:Class="PopupDemo.PopupPanel"
    xmlns="http://schemas.microsoft.com/winfx/2006/xaml/presentation"
    xmlns:x="http://schemas.microsoft.com/winfx/2006/xaml"
    xmlns:local="using:PopupDemo"
    xmlns:d="http://schemas.microsoft.com/expression/blend/2008"
    xmlns:mc="http://schemas.openxmlformats.org/markup-compatibility/2006"
    mc:Ignorable="d"
    d:DesignHeight="300"
    d:DesignWidth="400">

    <StackPanel
        Height="200"
        Width="200"
        Background="Wheat">
        <TextBlock
            Foreground="Black"
            Text="Welcome to my popup control!"
            FontSize="20" />
        <TextBlock
            Foreground="Black"
            Text="Push the button to close the popup"
            FontSize="10"
            Margin="0,10,0,0" />
        <Button
            Foreground="Black"
            Name="xClosePopup"
            Content="Close"
            Margin="0,10,0,0"
            Click="xClosePopup_Click_1" />
```

```
    </StackPanel>
</UserControl>
```

On the page that creates the popup, you add a Button to invoke the popup.

```
<StackPanel>
    <Button
        Name="xPopupButton"
        Click="xPopupButton_Click_1"
        Content="Show Popup" />
</StackPanel>
```

In the codebehind, you initialize a member of type Popup.

```
Popup popup = new Popup();
```

The event handler is then able to use this member to display the popup by checking the Popup property IsOpen and, assuming it is not open, creating a Child member of the type you created (your user control). You add the vertical and horizontal offset, and display the popup by setting IsOpen to true.

```
private void xPopupButton_Click_1( object sender, RoutedEventArgs e )
{
    if ( !popup.IsOpen )
    {
        popup.Child = new PopupPanel();
        popup.VerticalOffset = 200.0;
        popup.HorizontalOffset = 500.0;
        popup.IsOpen = true;
    }
}
```

In the event handler for the button within the popup, you obtain the original popup control (the parent to the user control) and set Popup.IsOpen to false, closing the popup.

```
private void xClosePopup_Click_1( object sender, RoutedEventArgs e )
{
    Popup PopupParent = Parent as Popup;
    PopupParent.IsOpen = false;
}
```

ProgressBar

A progress bar can be shown whenever you need to make the user aware that a lengthy process is proceeding. It can be run in either of two modes: indeterminate or determinate. The former shows dots that cycle through the control, the latter shows a bar that is filled proportionate to how much of the job is completed.

When you can break the process down into measurable chunks, the determinate approach provides more information to the user and is generally preferable; if you can't know how long remains, however, it is better to use the indeterminate approach.

In the following code, you create a ProgressBar class and set its IsDeterminate property to true if the corresponding checkbox is checked; this lets you display both modes of the ProgressBar. If you are showing a determinate ProgressBar, you fill the bar with the percentage entered into the corresponding TextBox, as shown in Figure 4-12.

```
<StackPanel
```

Figure 4-12. *A Determinate ProgressBar*

```xml
    Width="450"
    Height="150">
    <StackPanel
        Orientation="Horizontal"
        Margin="0,0,0,10">
        <TextBlock
            Text="Progress"
            VerticalAlignment="Center"
            Margin="0,0,10,0" />
        <Border
            BorderThickness="2"
            BorderBrush="#22FFFFFF"
            Padding="10">
            <ProgressBar
                x:Name="xProgressBar"
                IsIndeterminate="{Binding IsChecked, ElementName=xIndeterminate}"
                Width="100"
                Value="{Binding Text, ElementName=Value,
                    Converter={StaticResource StringToDoubleConverter}}" />
        </Border>
    </StackPanel>
    <StackPanel
        Orientation="Vertical"
        HorizontalAlignment="Center">
        <StackPanel
            Orientation="Horizontal">
            <CheckBox
                x:Name="xIndeterminate"
                Content="Indeterminate?"
                IsChecked="True" />
            <TextBlock
                Text="Percent:"
                VerticalAlignment="Center"
                Margin="10,0,0,0" />
            <TextBox
                x:Name="Value"
                Width="80"
                Height="30"
                Margin="10,0,0,0" />
        </StackPanel>
    </StackPanel>
</StackPanel>
```

ProgressRing

Either the indeterminate ProgressBar or the ProgressRing should be used when the user is aware she is waiting for something from the computer and it will take more than 2 seconds. The ProgressBar should be used in non-modal (non-blocking) situations, while the ProgressRing should be used with a modal (blocking) wait.

The ProgressRing has an IsActive property. When true, the ring spins; when false it is inert, as shown in the following code:

```
<StackPanel
    Width="450"
    Height="150">
    <StackPanel
        Orientation="Horizontal"
        Margin="0,0,0,10">
        <TextBlock
            Text="Progress"
            VerticalAlignment="Center"
            Margin="0,0,10,0" />
        <Border
            BorderThickness="2"
            BorderBrush="#22FFFFFF"
            Padding="10">
            <ProgressRing
                x:Name="xProgressBar"
                Width="100"
                IsActive="{Binding IsChecked, ElementName=xIsActive}" />
        </Border>
        <CheckBox
            Margin="5,0,0,0"
            x:Name="xIsActive"
            Content="Active?"
            IsChecked="True" />
    </StackPanel>
</StackPanel>
```

The result of setting IsActive to true is shown in Figure 4-13.

Figure 4-13. A ProgressRing set to IsActive

Tooltip

A tooltip "pops up" when the user hovers over an object with the mouse, or taps and holds the object with touch. The tooltip is typically added to provide additional or explanatory information. ToolTipService is a static class that provides static properties to allow the easy addition of a tooltip to a control. The following code illustrates adding a tooltip to an image with two additional lines of XAML (highlighted):

```
<StackPanel
    Grid.Row="2"
    Orientation="Horizontal"
    Margin="0,20,0,0">
    <TextBlock
        Text="Your Author: " />
    <Image
        x:Name="AuthorImage"
        Source="images/Jesse.jpg"
        Width="400"
        Height="500"
        Stretch="UniformToFill"
        Margin="10,0,0,0"
        ToolTipService.ToolTip="Your Author"
        ToolTipService.Placement="Right" />
</StackPanel>
```

Figure 4-14 shows the tooltip in action.

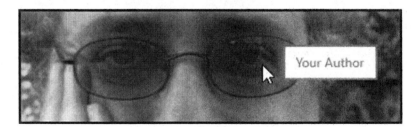

Figure 4-14. Helpful tooltip

■ ■ ■

CHAPTER 5

Styles and Templates

The most common way for programmers new to XAML to set styles on their controls is with inline styles. In other words, the styling information (font size, font family, etc.) is set as attributes on the control itself, as shown in the following code:

```
<Button
    FontSize="24"
    Height="60"
    Width="180"
    Content="Click Me!" />
```

While this works well in small demonstration programs, it gets tedious when setting the same styling information on dozens of controls. Worse, if you decide to modify the style (and you *will* modify the style!), you must replicate the changes on all of the dozens of controls.

The solution to this problem is to create styles as resources. Styles have a target type and a key, and you can then associate a style with a control with one line of XAML, as shown in the following example:

```
<Page.Resources>
    <Style
        TargetType="Button"
        x:Key="ButtonStyle">
        <Setter
            Property="FontSize"
            Value="24" />
        <Setter
            Property="Height"
            Value="60" />
        <Setter
            Property="Width"
            Value="180" />

    </Style>
</Page.Resources>

<Grid
    Background="{StaticResource ApplicationPageBackgroundThemeBrush}">
    <StackPanel>
        <Button
```

```
                Style="{StaticResource ButtonStyle}"
                Content="Click Me!" />
            <Button
                Style="{StaticResource ButtonStyle}"
                Content="No! Click Me!" />

        </StackPanel>
    </Grid>
```

You *could* define the style inline, but in this case you've defined a reusable style in the Page Resources section. Any button on the page can set its font size, height, and width just by setting its style to this style resource, using the assigned key ButtonStyle. In Figure 5-1, you see an example of two buttons doing just that in the stack panel; they each use the same style and so each have the same width, height, and font size.

Figure 5-1. *Defining styles*

You can set as many properties and corresponding values as you like in a style.

Based on Styles

You can create new styles based on existing styles, overriding one or more properties and adding new properties. For example, you could create an Urgent button based on the ButtonStyle shown above, but with the letters in yellow, as shown in the following code:

```
<Page.Resources>
    <Style
        TargetType="Button"
        x:Key="ButtonStyle">
        <Setter
            Property="FontSize"
            Value="24" />
        <Setter
            Property="Height"
            Value="60" />
        <Setter
            Property="Width"
            Value="180" />
    </Style>
    <Style TargetType="Button" x:Key="UrgentButtonStyle" BasedOn="{StaticResource ButtonStyle}">
        <Setter
```

```
                Property="Foreground"
                Value="Yellow" />
        </Style>
</Page.Resources>

<Grid
    Background="{StaticResource ApplicationPageBackgroundThemeBrush}">
    <StackPanel>
        <Button
            Style="{StaticResource ButtonStyle}"
            Content="Click Me!" />
        <Button
            Style="{StaticResource UrgentButtonStyle}"
            Content="No! Click Me!" />

    </StackPanel>
</Grid>
```

In this simple example, a second style, UrgentButtonStyle, is based on the original ButtonStyle, but a new property is added (Foreground). Using "Based on" you can create an entire hierarchy of related styles.

Implicit Styles

So what if you want to apply a given style to every button on your page but don't want to define the style in each button? In that case, you can create an *implicit style*. Implicit styles are defined exactly like explicit styles, except that there is no key; every control of the target type is assigned the implicit style, … implicitly, as illustrated in the following code:

```
<Page.Resources>
    <Style
        TargetType="Button">
        <Setter
            Property="FontSize"
            Value="24" />
        <Setter
            Property="Height"
            Value="60" />
        <Setter
            Property="Width"
            Value="180" />
    </Style>
</Page.Resources>

<Grid
    Background="{StaticResource ApplicationPageBackgroundThemeBrush}">
    <StackPanel>
        <Button
            Content="Click Me!" />
        <Button
            Content="No! Click Me!" />
        <Button
```

```
                Content="Thing 1" />
        <Button
                Content="Thing 2" />

    </StackPanel>
</Grid>
```

Note that the style does not have a key, and none of the buttons set their style. They are assigned the new style implicitly specifically because it *doesn't* have a key, based on the TargetType. Figure 5-2 shows the result.

Figure 5-2. Implicit styles

Templates

While styles can give you a great deal of flexibility, they can only go so far. If you want to take full control over the appearance of a control, you will want to provide a custom template. Every control in Windows 8 is "lookless" in that it has no inherent appearance. Its appearance is controlled by a template, either the template created by Microsoft or the template created by you.

To see this, let's create a template to make your buttons round and blue. To do so, open Expression Blend and create a new project. Drag a button onto the design surface and right-click the button, choosing Edit Template ➤ Create Empty, as shown in Figure 5-3.

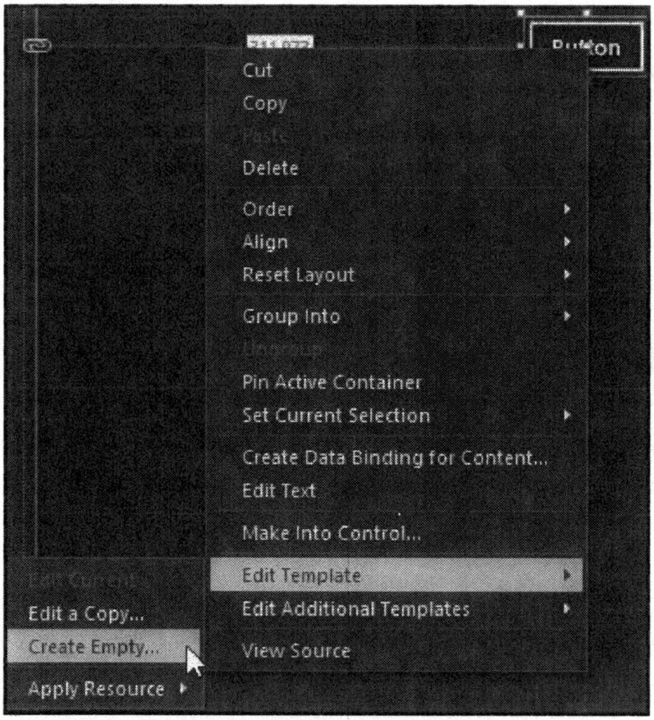

Figure 5-3. Creating an empty template

A dialog box will open and ask you to name the template and set its scope. Your choices are

- Application (any page in this project)

- This document (this page)

- Resource dictionary (a reusable DLL that just contains resources for use across projects)

Choose Application, as shown in Figure 5-4.

Create ControlTemplate Resource   ×

Name (Key)

◉ RoundButtonTemplate

◯ Apply to all

Define in

◉ Application

◯ This document   Page: <no name>

◯ Resource dictionary   StandardStyles.xaml

[OK]   [Cancel]

Figure 5-4. Setting the scope of the template

This will put you in the template editor, creating a new template for buttons. In the center of the template is a small grid. Click on the grid, and in the Properties window, set its size to 100x100. Drag an ellipse into the grid, and set its size to 80x80, centered and with no margins, as shown in Figure 5-5.

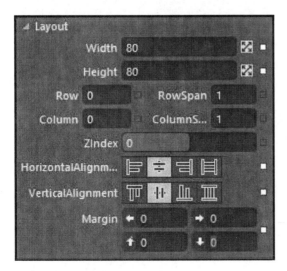

Figure 5-5. Setting the size of the ellipse

Set the fill color of the ellipse to a light blue. Drag a TextBlock into the grid, center it, and set its contents to Click Me. You now have an ellipse with the words "Click Me" superimposed above it. That is your template for the button.

To exit the template editor, double-click on MainPage.xaml at the top of the designer. You will exit the template designer and be back in the page designer.

Drag a second button onto the page. Click on the Resources tab and expand App.xaml. You'll see your newly minted template, which is called RoundButtonTemplate in this example (see Figure 5-6).

Figure 5-6. *The new template*

Click and drag RoundButtonTemplate onto the new button. Notice that the cursor now has a + sign (see Figure 5-7).

Figure 5-7. *Setting the scope of the template*

When you let go of the mouse, a menu will appear where you are dropping the template. Select Template to add the template to this button (as shown in Figure 5-8) and hey! Presto! The button changes to your template shape.

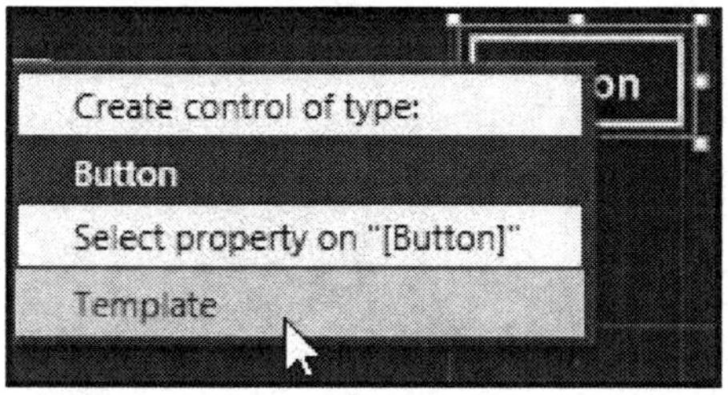

Figure 5-8. *Selecting the Template option*

Click F5 to run the application and your two templated buttons will appear as shown in Figure 5-9.

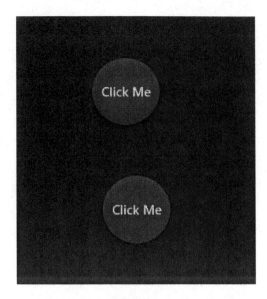

Figure 5-9. The new buttons!

Your new buttons will still respond to click events (they *are* buttons), even though you have dramatically changed their appearance. To prove it, close the application in Blend and open it in Visual Studio. Put the buttons into a StackPanel and add a TextBlock to display a message. Finally, add a Click event handler to the second button as follows:

```
<StackPanel>
    <Button
        Content="Button"
        HorizontalAlignment="Left"
        VerticalAlignment="Top"
        Template="{StaticResource RoundButtonTemplate}" />
    <Button
        Content="Button"
        HorizontalAlignment="Left"
        VerticalAlignment="Top"
        Template="{StaticResource RoundButtonTemplate}"
        Click="Button_Click_1" />
    <TextBlock
        Margin="20"
        FontSize="40"
        Name="Msg"
        Text="Ready" />
</StackPanel>
```

The event handler for the Click event will just update the TextBlock, as shown in the following code:

```
private void Button_Click_1(object sender, Windows.UI.Xaml.RoutedEventArgs e)
{
        Msg.Text = "Clicked!";
}
```

When you click on the second button, voila! the text changes, as shown in Figure 5-10.

Figure 5-10. *Changing text*

While the buttons do still respond to click events, they do not give the positive feedback of appearing to be depressed when you click on them. To accomplish that, you need to know about animation and visual states, the topics of the next chapter.

■ ■ ■

CHAPTER 6

Animation and Visual State

One of the things that sharply distinguish XAML from simpler markup languages such as HTML is that XAML supports declarative animation. That is, you can indicate a property and the change you'd like to have happen to that property over a set amount of time. For example, you might indicate that the height of an object show grow from 45 to 90 pixels over 1 second.

XAML animation is managed by Storyboards. A Storyboard is a named set of XAML declarations that detail the steps of an animation. A Storyboard has a key so that you can refer to it programmatically, and it has within it XAML objects called animations. Each animation is named for the type of property it affects, so DoubleAnimation affects a property of type Double, PointAnimation affects points, etc.

From-To Animation

The simplest kind of animation is a From-To, in which you specify the starting and ending value of a property. For example, you can define a DoubleAnimation to change the font size of a text block from a value of 9 (quite small) to a value of 96 (quite large). You can specify how long the animation is to run (e.g., two seconds) and Windows will interpolate all the intervening sizes for you, giving you a smooth animation so that at one second the font size is half way between 9 and 96 (52.5).

```
<Page>
  <Page.Resources>
    <Storyboard x:Key="TextEnlarger">
        <DoubleAnimation
                        Storyboard.TargetName="displayText"
                        Storyboard.TargetProperty="FontSize"
                        EnableDependentAnimation="True"
                        From="9"
                        To="96"
                        Duration="0:0:2" />
    </Storyboard>
</Page.Resources>

<Grid Background="{StaticResource ApplicationPageBackgroundThemeBrush}">
    <StackPanel Margin="50">
        <TextBlock Name="displayText"
                    Text="Hello World!" />
        <Button Content="Do It"
```

```
          Click="Button_Click_1" />

    </StackPanel>
</Grid>
</Page>
```

In the DoubleAnimation, you declare the TargetName (the name of the item you are animating) and the TargetProperty (the property on that object that you are animating). You declare the From and To value and the Duration in the format hours:minutes:seconds. (You can declare hundredths of a second by using a dot after seconds, and you can declare days by using a dot before hours.) Because this animation affects the UI you also need to set EnableDependentAnimation to true, because the default is not to enable animation on the UI.

■ **Note**   In rare cases, you may have an animation that does not affect the UI at all, but is used as a timer or for other internal purposes. Most animations affect the UI, as that is what is generally meant by "animation."

When you click the button, the event handler is called, like so:

```
private void Button_Click_1( object sender, RoutedEventArgs e )
{
    var sb = Resources["TextEnlarger"] as Storyboard;
    sb.Begin();
}
```

The Storyboard runs, setting the font to 9 and expanding it to 96 over the course of two seconds and then stopping. If you change the Duration to 4 seconds, it will do the same work but at half the speed. You can leave out the From value and it will start at the current font size and expand to 96. You can also add an AutoReverse attribute to the DoubleAnimation element, which will cause the animation to finish and then reverse course, descending to a font size of 9.

```
<DoubleAnimation Storyboard.TargetName="displayText"
                 Storyboard.TargetProperty="FontSize"
                 EnableDependentAnimation="True"
                 From="9"
                 To="96"
                 Duration="0:0:2"
                 AutoReverse="True"/>
```

Notice that AutoReverse doubles the time for the entire animation to run.

Key-frame Animation

A second type of animation is called key-frame. Rather than simply specifying the starting and ending points of your animation, you can specify the exact values at different times, allowing you greater control over the animation. If you have a value set at one second and a value set at two seconds, Windows will interpolate the values between the key frames to provide a smooth animation (unless you specify that you want to jump from one value to the next with no intervening values).

While you certainly *can* continue to write your storyboards in XAML directly, it is far easier to create your animation in Blend for Visual Studio and then examine the XAML that is output by Blend. For example, open Blend and create a new project called KeyFrameAnimation. Drag an ellipse onto the artboard. Click on the plus sign to create a new Storyboard, as shown in Figure 6-1.

Figure 6-1. New Storyboard

Name your new Storyboard BouncingBall. Change your view by clicking on Windows ➤ Workspaces ➤ Animation. The Animation window opens at the bottom of the screen. With the yellow line on 0, click the Record Keyframe icon, as shown in Figure 6-2.

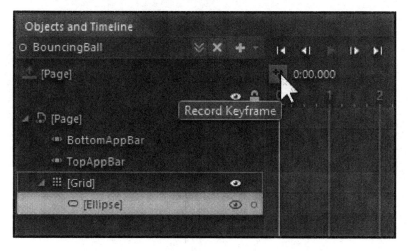

Figure 6-2. Record the keyframe

This records your starting point. Now click on the 1 second mark and move the ellipse to the bottom of the screen and then click the Record Keyframe icon. This means that after 1 second, the ball should have moved all the way to the bottom.

Move the timeline to 2 seconds and move the ellipse to a new position. Do the same at 3 seconds. Now click the Play button (above the timeline) and watch the ellipse move.

In the upper left corner you can see a red dot that says recording is on. Click it to turn recording off. Switch from Design view to XAML view by clicking the Code button in the upper right corner of the Design window. Your XAML will look something like this:

```
<Page.Resources>
        <Storyboard x:Name="BouncingBall">
                <DoubleAnimationUsingKeyFrames Storyboard.TargetProperty="(UIElement.
RenderTransform).(CompositeTransform.TranslateX)" Storyboard.TargetName="ellipse">
                        <EasingDoubleKeyFrame KeyTime="0" Value="0"/>
```

```
                    <EasingDoubleKeyFrame KeyTime="0:0:1" Value="-10.028"/>
                    <EasingDoubleKeyFrame KeyTime="0:0:2" Value="246.236"/>
                    <EasingDoubleKeyFrame KeyTime="0:0:3" Value="436.763"/>
            </DoubleAnimationUsingKeyFrames>
            <DoubleAnimationUsingKeyFrames Storyboard.TargetProperty="(UIElement.
RenderTransform).(CompositeTransform.TranslateY)" Storyboard.TargetName="ellipse">
                    <EasingDoubleKeyFrame KeyTime="0" Value="0"/>
                    <EasingDoubleKeyFrame KeyTime="0:0:1" Value="593.865"/>
                    <EasingDoubleKeyFrame KeyTime="0:0:2" Value="-45.681"/>
                    <EasingDoubleKeyFrame KeyTime="0:0:3" Value="606.122"/>
            </DoubleAnimationUsingKeyFrames>
        </Storyboard>
</Page.Resources>

<Grid Background="{StaticResource ApplicationPageBackgroundThemeBrush}">
        <Ellipse x:Name="ellipse" Fill="#FFF4F4F5" HorizontalAlignment="Left" Height="100"
Margin="57,62,0,0" Stroke="Black" VerticalAlignment="Top" Width="100"
RenderTransformOrigin="0.5,0.5">
                <Ellipse.RenderTransform>
                    <CompositeTransform/>
                </Ellipse.RenderTransform>
        </Ellipse>

</Grid>
```

Let's unpack this code and see what is going on. It begins with the declaration of the Storyboard within the Page Resources.

```
<Page.Resources>
        <Storyboard x:Name="BouncingBall">
```

The next line declares a DoubleAnimation using key frames, which is just what you want. The TargetProperty may look a little odd, however.

```
Storyboard.TargetProperty="(UIElement.RenderTransform).(CompositeTransform.TranslateX)"
Storyboard.TargetName="ellipse">
```

All this is telling you is that the target property of this animation is TranslateX. A translation is a movement of the object and this is movement on the x axis. All of the values, therefore, will be locations on the x axis as the ellipse moves across the page.

You then see four EasingDoubleKeyFrame entries. We'll come back to what easing is all about later in this chapter, but what you see are times and values. At each of these times, the X value will be set to the corresponding value.

```
<EasingDoubleKeyFrame KeyTime="0" Value="0"/>
<EasingDoubleKeyFrame KeyTime="0:0:1" Value="-10.028"/>
<EasingDoubleKeyFrame KeyTime="0:0:2" Value="246.236"/>
<EasingDoubleKeyFrame KeyTime="0:0:3" Value="436.763"/>
```

That concludes the first DoubleAnimation, which is immediately followed by a second DoubleAnimation using key frames to affect the position on the y axis.

```
<DoubleAnimationUsingKeyFrames Storyboard.TargetProperty="(UIElement.RenderTransform).
(CompositeTransform.TranslateY)" Storyboard.TargetName="ellipse">
```

In the body of the XAML (outside the resource) the ellipse is defined, along with the information needed to transform that ellipse through the animation. The purpose of a `CompositeTransform` is to allow the object to be transformed in two or more ways at one time. In your case, you are translating (moving) it on both the x and y axis.

Most of the time, you can use Blend to set up your animations and not worry about the XAML that is output for you; it will work as expected. When it doesn't, rather than hacking the XAML directly, you are most often better off opening the project in Blend again and fixing it interactively. But you are always free to tinker directly with the XAML, and the tools (Blend, Visual Studio) will figure out what changes you have made without a problem.

Easing

Imagine you are watching a film of an old-fashioned steam locomotive and train at the station. You can hear the hissing and the clanging as the train starts up. Suddenly, and without buildup, it is travelling at 60 MPH. You reject this instantly as cartoonish. Trains do not behave that way; they start off slow and build to a speed, then they slow to a stop. This is true of many things in real life; though the transformations in speed may be more subtle and quicker, things don't go from zero to full speed and back.

Easing is a mechanism to make your animation smoother and more realistic. Rather than moving an item instantly, it allows the item to build up speed and/or taper off. To see this, create a new application in Blend called `EasingDemo`. Draw a rectangle on the artboard, and set a key frame at 0 seconds with the rectangle at the far left of the screen. Set a second key frame at 1 second with the rectangle at the far right. Note that the red recording indicator is on in the upper left corner of the artboard. Click it to turn off recording. The Properties window will now show the Easing functions, as shown in Figure 6-3.

Figure 6-3. Easing functions

Easing is described as in, out, or in/out. Easing *in* affects the start of the animation, while easing *out* affects the end of the animation. The drawings give you an idea of what the easing will do. For example, consider the circle easing. You can see that it will start slowly and then rapidly accelerate. Out will do the opposite, starting quick and rapidly decelerating. Try different easing functions to see the effect on your animation. A very common and satisfying choice is the exponential in/out easing function, but the bounce function is great fun.

View State

Return to the template buttons you created in the previous chapter. Open the template and click on the States tab, as shown in Figure 6-4.

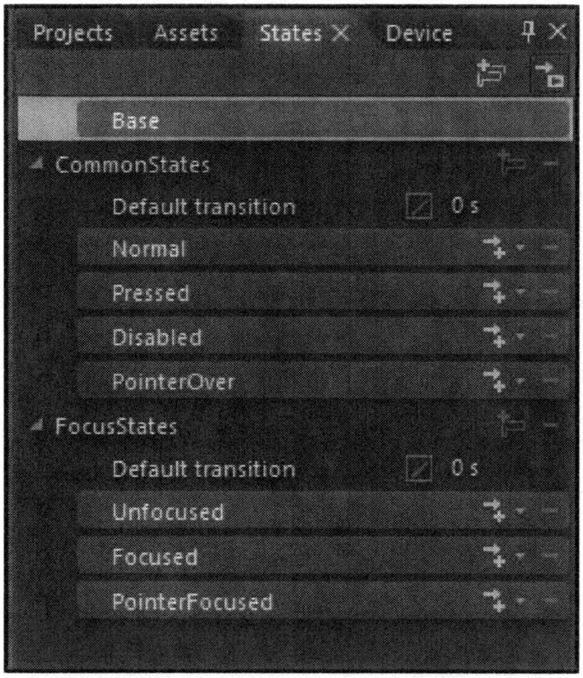

Figure 6-4. *Easing options*

Take a look at the States window. This displays the view states. The view state affects how the control appears based on its state. An example of a state is whether or not the control has the focus, or whether or not a button is being pressed. As the state changes, the view will change to reflect the change in state. This change is accomplished through animation controlled by the View State Manager.

There are a few things to notice right away. First, the control has a Base state, and then there are two state groups: CommonStates and FocusStates. A control can be in any one state from each state group at any given time. Thus, it can have the focus (Focused) and be pressed, but it can't have the focus and be unfocused at the same time.

In the previous chapter, you were not getting visual feedback when the button was pressed. All you need to do now is to click on the Pressed state. That will put you into recording mode, and you can record the animation you want to run when the item is pressed.

Notice that the frame has turned red. While it is red, you are recording all the changes that should occur when the control goes into the Pressed state. Expand the timeline and create a key frame at time zero for the ellipse. Next, move the time line to ½ second and open the Transforms section and find the scale transform. Set the ellipse's x and y sizes both to .75, as shown in Figure 6-5. Thus, in over half a second the ellipse will shrink by 25% when the Pressed state is entered.

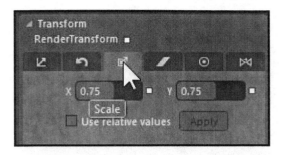

Figure 6-5. Setting the size of the ellipse

Do the same thing for the TextBlock that has the Click Me text. Also, while the TextBlock is clicked, click the Rotate transform (just to the left of the scale) and set it to 45 degrees. This will twist the text while it shrinks. Click the red button to turn recording off, as shown in Figure 6-6.

Figure 6-6. Turn off the recording

Run the application. You should see your nice round button; when you press on it, it should shrink and twist. This is the power of combining the View State Manager with animations.

You may want to set animations for other view states. Notice that there is a PointerOver view state, which works well when you use a mouse or other pointer, but has no effect when using your fingers.

Let's look at the XAML you've created.

```
<VisualStateManager.VisualStateGroups>
   <VisualStateGroup x:Name="CommonStates">
      <VisualState x:Name="Normal">
         <Storyboard/>
      </VisualState>
      <VisualState x:Name="Pressed">
         <Storyboard>
            <DoubleAnimationUsingKeyFrames
            Storyboard.TargetProperty="(UIElement.RenderTransform).(CompositeTransform.ScaleX)"
            Storyboard.TargetName="ellipse">
               <EasingDoubleKeyFrame KeyTime="0" Value="1"/>
               <EasingDoubleKeyFrame KeyTime="0:0:1" Value="0.75"/>
            </DoubleAnimationUsingKeyFrames>
            <DoubleAnimationUsingKeyFrames
            Storyboard.TargetProperty="(UIElement.RenderTransform).(CompositeTransform.ScaleY)"
            Storyboard.TargetName="ellipse">
               <EasingDoubleKeyFrame KeyTime="0" Value="1"/>
```

```
                    <EasingDoubleKeyFrame KeyTime="0:0:1" Value="0.75"/>
                </DoubleAnimationUsingKeyFrames>
                <DoubleAnimationUsingKeyFrames
                Storyboard.TargetProperty="(UIElement.RenderTransform).(CompositeTransform.ScaleX)"
                Storyboard.TargetName="textBlock">
                    <EasingDoubleKeyFrame KeyTime="0" Value="1"/>
                    <EasingDoubleKeyFrame KeyTime="0:0:1" Value="0.75"/>
                </DoubleAnimationUsingKeyFrames>
                <DoubleAnimationUsingKeyFrames
                Storyboard.TargetProperty="(UIElement.RenderTransform).(CompositeTransform.ScaleY)"
                Storyboard.TargetName="textBlock">
                    <EasingDoubleKeyFrame KeyTime="0" Value="1"/>
                    <EasingDoubleKeyFrame KeyTime="0:0:1" Value="0.75"/>
                </DoubleAnimationUsingKeyFrames>
                <DoubleAnimationUsingKeyFrames
                Storyboard.TargetProperty="(UIElement.RenderTransform).(CompositeTransform.
Rotation)"
                Storyboard.TargetName="textBlock">
                    <EasingDoubleKeyFrame KeyTime="0" Value="0"/>
                    <EasingDoubleKeyFrame KeyTime="0:0:1" Value="45"/>
                </DoubleAnimationUsingKeyFrames>
            </Storyboard>
        </VisualState>
        <VisualState x:Name="Disabled"/>
        <VisualState x:Name="PointerOver"/>
    </VisualStateGroup>
    <VisualStateGroup x:Name="FocusStates">
        <VisualState x:Name="Focused"/>
        <VisualState x:Name="PointerFocused"/>
    </VisualStateGroup>
</VisualStateManager.VisualStateGroups>
```

You begin with the declaration of the Visual State Manager VisualStateGroups. Each VisualStateGroup has a set of visual states (e.g., Focused, Unfocused, etc.) For most of these states, you have not put in any transformations or animations and so they are empty. The one that is not empty is Pressed.

Pressed consists of a storyboard with a series of DoubleAnimationUsingKeyframes. Each targets a different property: first the x and y property of the ellipse, then the x and y property of the TextBlock, and finally the rotation of the TextBlock.

Once you understand what the View States are for and what the animations are doing, the code becomes very readable. Again, you *can* write all this by hand, but that is error prone and tedious. I highly recommend using Blend for Visual Studio whenever you have to add animations.

Much of the animation in Windows is triggered by a change to the view. This becomes very important in Windows 8 programming because the View State Manager handles the transition in state from full screen to snapped view, etc.

Index

A, B

Animation and visual state, 71
  easing, 75
    functions, 76
    key frame, 75
    options, 77
  from-to, 71
    DoubleAnimation, 71, 72
    TargetName, 72
  key-frame, 72
    CompositeTransform, 75
    design, 73–74
    easing, 74
    record, 73
    storyboard, 73
  view state, 76
    easing options, 77
    off record, 78
    PointerOver, 78–79
    run, 78–79
    size setting, 78
    visual state manager, 79
ApplicationPageBackgroundThemeBrush, 3

C

Controls, XAML, 37
  contents, 37, 43
    action, toggle switch, 45
    add checkbox, 44
    adding items, 46–47
    AppBar, 47–50
    button images, 48–49
    canvas, shapes, 52
    CheckBox, 44
    child member, 57
    class, AppBar, 49–50
    collecting items, 47
    collection, FlipView, 55
    ellipse and rectangle, 51–52
    event handler, 50
    FlipView, 54–55
    GridView, 46–47
    image, 54
    IsActive, ProgressRing, 59
    ListView, 46–47
    ListView element, 46
    MediaElement, 55–56
    path, 52–53
    path canvas, 53
    popup, 56–57
    Popup.IsOpen, 57
    presentation, 53–60
    ProgressBar, 57–58
    ProgressRing, 59
    property, 43
    Push me!, 43
    RadioButton, 45–46
    shapes, 51–53
    slider, 53–54
    text and checkbox, 44
    TextBlock, 50
    TextBlock, slider, 54
    ToggleSwitch, 45
    ToolTipService, 60
  selection, 41
    button, 41
    event handler, button, 42
    HyperlinkButton, 41
    ToggleButton, 42
TextControls, 37
  await key, 40
  file picker, 40
  in a button, 38

Controls, TextControls (*cont.*)
LostFocus event, 39
PasswordBox, 38–39
reveal button, 38
RichEditBox, 39–41
rich text, 39
.rtf form, 41

■ D-O

Data binding, 17
and data conversion, 23
IValueConverter, 23
Page.Resource, 23–24
and INotifyPropertyChanged, 19
class implement, 20–21
event handler, 21
implement, 19
simulation, 20
modes, 19
ProcessRing, 22
to lists, 24
ComboBox, 26
data source, 24
DataTemplate, 25
ItemTemplate, 26
to objects, 17
class properties, 18
DataContext, 18–19
POCO, 18
TextBlocks, 17
to other elements, 22

■ P, Q, R

Panels, 27
abstract base class, 27
border, 35
class hierarchy, 27
canvas, 28
elements, 28
objects, 28–29
overlaped objects, 29
properties, 28
rectangles, object, 30
ZIndex property, 29–30
grid, 31
adding objects, 32–33
define, 31
output, 33
placing objects, 33
row definition, 32

size, 31
start sizing, 31
stack, 30
items, 30–31
orientation, 31
WrapGrid, 34
ItemsPanel, 34
output, 35

■ S

Styles, 61
attributes, 61
define, 62
implicit, 63–64
new styles, 62–63
resources, 61

■ T, U, V, W

Templates, 61, 64
empty, 64–65
new, 66–67
new buttons, 67–68
option selection, 67
scope setting, 65–66
setting size, 66
text change, 69

■ X, Y, Z

XAML, 1
programming, 1
auto sizing, 9
class name, 9
improved grid, 11
code declaration, 7
event handling, 6–7
example, 4
first application, 1–4
forms, stack, 4
grid, 3
grid dimensions, 7
layout improvement, 7–11
layout sizing, 8
methods, event handling, 6
namespace telerik, 3
parameter, event, 7
results and ratios, 8
RoutedEventArgs, 7
row and column, grid, 9–11
solution explorer, 2
stack panel, 4–6

TextBlock element, 3–4
    text property, 6
    Visual studio project, 2
    XML namespaces, 3
properties and controls, 14
    attributes, 14–15
    excerpt for TextBlock, 15
    grid, 14
    toolbox property, 15
Windows 8 and layout, 11
    alignment, 13

    conventions, 13–14
    font sizes, 13
    gridlines, 14
    HorizontalAlignment, 13
    margin setting, 12
    padding, 12–13
    position and size, 11–12
    size allocation, 12
    space availability, 12
    VerticalAlignment, 13

CPSIA information can be obtained at www.ICGtesting.com
Printed in the USA
LVOW112256051112

306014LV00005B/68/P